Dividend Growth Investing

The Wealth Building Machine

2019

First Edition

Published by Gene Giordano

ISBN: 9781796300772

Dividend Growth Investing

The Wealth Building

Machine

All commentary throughout this book is from the perspective of Gene Giordano. **At this time, I would like to make an honorary mention of my co-author and good friend Patrick D'Onofrio. Patrick played an integral part in the overall construction, editing, and design of this book.**

This book has been dedicated to my beloved, long lasting clients. Thank you all for instilling your trust and support in me for the past 25 years

–Gene Giordano

Table of Contents

Foreword………..………………………………………………………........3

About the Author……………………....…....……………….....……....8

Section 1: Dividend Growth Investing

Chapter 1: An Introduction to Dividend Growth Investing……....…..11

Section 2: The Threats to our Financial Wealth

Chapter 2: Understated Inflation and Low Interest Rate…..………....29

Chapter 3: Longevity Risk……………………….....…………....39

Chapter 4: Taxes……………………....………………...…….…61

Chapter 5: The Media and the Investor…………………………….....85

Section 3: The Solutions

Chapter 6: Enhanced Investment Returns…………………….…....100

Chapter 7: The Power of Yield on Cost……………….....………....122

Chapter 8: Principal Preservation..……………………....…….….141

Chapter 9: Quantitative Approach……………………...…………....162

Section 4: The Conclusion

Chapter 10: Bringing it all Together…..……………………....….174

Foreword

For over a quarter of a century, daily conversations on the topic of investing have taken up much of my time. From ordinary working class citizens to celebrities, from politicians to successful real estate investors; one thing I have learned through these conversations is simple; **everyone has an opinion on the stock market.**

Through the different opinions, the different perspectives, and even the different strategies highlighting how to "beat the market", I found one common thread amongst these conversations. **Almost every individual that I conversed with shared a common misconception.**

This misconception is not minor, nor would I consider it to be moderately significant. **Instead, I strongly believe this misconception is, and has been, the largest threat to the livelihood of people around the world.**

It has become conventional wisdom that the ultimate purpose of the stock market is to make "extra" money. People perceive "investing" as a non-obligatory action, but instead, as an activity for those who wish to gamble a small portion of their money away in return for the opportunity to reap large rewards. In my opinion, **this notion is single-handedly one of the largest contributors to restricting a majority of people from achieving financial freedom.**

What is financial freedom you might ask? Financial freedom means waking up to go to work because you *want* to, not because you *have* to. It means being able to spend more time with family and friends. It means living day to day knowing you can retire at any given moment and enjoy the remainder of your days worry free.

So why are so many individuals who make the average salary struggling to come even remotely close to achieving financial freedom? Well, for one, the Investment Media and governments around the world have done nothing but encourage this false phenomenon of investing by publishing news stories and creating policies that focus on benefiting the insiders of these institutions at the expense of providing misinformation to society. For example, from childhood, the Media as well as the laws constructed by the government have taught us that in order to be successful, we must:

- 1) Finish high school
- 2) Go to post-secondary to earn a degree
- 2) Get a good job based on the degree

- 3) Save money from your job to buy a house
- 4) Save money for retirement

Notice how, in this classic scenario, the "successful person's" employment income is responsible for paying for their degree, purchasing their home, funding theirs and their family's lifestyle, and setting aside enough money so that, when they retire, they can still afford to survive? While this is what society has been led to believe is optimal, I, along with people who have achieved, or are on the path to achieve, financial freedom, believe there is a better way. As I will explain throughout this book, it is imperative to **view employment income as a supplement to fuel our contributions to investment accounts rather than as our sole source of income.**

If I have not already emphasised just how important investing is, let me say this; I believe not only should society place a greater emphasis on investing, but also, we should consider it to be of equal importance to items like food, education, shelter, and employment. **In other words, investing must be viewed as a necessity rather than a luxury.**

Throughout this book, I will introduce a list of threats to our financial wealth that can only be eliminated through the power of generating a sufficient return from our investments. My hope is that being able to recognize the significant negative impact these threats pose on our financial wealth will influence readers to realize that the societal norm of viewing investing as a "bonus" to employment income is entirely flawed.

Twenty-five years of experience in the Financial Services Industry has led me to become a disciple of *Dividend Growth Investing*. This long-term, conservative investment philosophy is, in my opinion, the most effective strategy we can use to protect ourselves from the many threats to our financial wealth. Through this book, we will see how each of the many unique qualities that make up Dividend Growth Investing provides a solution to each potential threat.

As mentioned, understanding the threats to our financial wealth will make it clear that the motivation for achieving long-term returns on our capital should not arise solely from the desire to simply maximize our wealth. **Instead, the purpose of striving to achieve above average returns**

is to create a defense mechanism that will protect us from the ultimate risk: not being able to achieve financial freedom. The sooner this concept becomes evident, the sooner the investor can truly maximize the power of Dividend Growth Investing.

About The Author

Gene Giordano, CFP, CIM

Gene entered the Wealth Management industry in 1988 when he co-founded an integrated full-service investment firm by the name of **Strategic Financial Management Group Inc.** During this period, Gene and his team provided clients with tax minimization solutions, investment diversification services, and estate and retirement planning services. His investment team was the recipient of the *Investment Team of the Year* award for four consecutive years. This highly coveted award recognizes those who provide clients with comprehensive investment planning, clear and effective client communication, clarity, transparency, and outstanding performance.

Prior to joining the Wealth Management industry, Gene worked for a **Toronto-based real estate organization**, specializing in the selection and acquisition of quality commercial and industrial income properties across North America. This position was held until 1990.

Today, Gene focuses on providing sophisticated wealth management solutions for over 200 families, business owners, and professionals. **With more than 25 years of experience in real estate and Wealth Management, Gene prides himself on having mastered an in-depth, proprietary strategy for solving all of the major issues faced by families, business owners, and professionals.**

Gene is actively involved in community fundraising, particularly for *Hospital for Sick Children*, *Friends of Amani*, *Villa Charities* and *The Etobicoke Sports Hall of Fame*, where he serves as Governor. He is a past Board Member and fundraising Chair for *Dorothy Ley Hospice*, an organization that helps people and their families who are facing a progressive, life-threatening illness. Gene enjoys running marathons, cycling, reading and spending time with his wife and two daughters.

Section One:

Dividend Growth Investing

Chapter One

An Introduction to Dividend Growth Investing

What is a Dividend?

Once every two weeks, I am presented with a different atmosphere at my office. The secretaries are pleased to see me, the associates seem more motivated, and even the manager himself seems a bit more cheerful. Now, if I can assure you of one thing, it is this: the unusual behaviour exhibited by my colleagues on this special day has nothing to do with me. Rather, this wonderful day provides validation that the work they do is appreciated for the value it adds to the firm. Have you still not guessed what day it is? Well, if you guessed "payday", you are absolutely correct.

A dividend paid to holders of a company's shares represents a part of the firm's after tax profits which the firm chooses to share with its owners, the shareholders. When it comes to deciding how to make use of a company's profits, there are generally three basic options available to the firm's board of directors:

1. Net profits can be reinvested into projects which the firm feels will be profitable; or
2. Net profits can be held in cash within the corporation; or
3. Net profits can be distributed to shareholders in the form of a dividend.

Corporations that choose to distribute dividends to shareholders generally do so four times per year. Each company sets its own payout schedule and determines the dates on which the dividend payments will be made. Some companies may even pay a special, one-time dividend every so often if they are in the position of holding excess cash with no immediate plans for deployment.

To summarize, **dividends are the portion of a firm's after-tax profits which they choose to distribute to shareholders in the form of cash**. With that being said, why should an investor care about dividends and where do they fall under the realm of **total return**?

When an investor purchases a share in a company, their total return is derived from two components:

1. Share price appreciation; and
2. Dividend income.

Let us assume an investor purchases 10,000 shares of Company A at $10 per share. Company A pays a quarterly cash dividend of $0.05/share, equating to an annual dividend yield of 2%. After one year, the investor revisits their portfolio to evaluate the performance. At this point, shares in Company A are trading at $13. Over the course of the year, what was the investor's total return?

Remember, as previously mentioned, the investor's total return is derived from both share price appreciation and dividend income. Therefore, in this scenario, the investor's total return would be calculated as follows:

Share Price Appreciation

10,000 Shares at $10 per share at Beginning of Year 1 = $100,000

10,000 Shares at $13 per share at End of Year 1 = $130,000

Unrealized Gain = $30,000

Dividend Income

Number of Shares = 10,000

Quarterly Dividend Income per Share = $0.05

Annual Dividend Income per Share = $0.20

Annual Dividend Income = $2,000

Total Return

Return from Share Price Appreciation = $30,000

Return from Dividend Income = $2,000

Total Return = $32,000

When we compare the return generated from Dividend Income to the return derived from Share Price Appreciation, investors must be aware of two notable differences:

- 1) Dividend Income is calculated independent of a company's share price. Therefore, in our previous example, even if Company A's share price had decreased to $8 at the end of the first year, the investor would still have received four $500 quarterly dividend payments, representing an Annual Dividend Income of $2,000.

- 2) Dividend Income is paid in cash directly to the investor's account on the Dividend Payout Date. However, a return generated from Share Price Appreciation is not available in cash. Instead, it becomes "locked in" only when the investor decides to sell their shares. Until that time, the return is marked as "unrealized" to reflect the fact that it is likely to fluctuate as the company's share price increases or decreases.

As a summary, the return generated by dividends is independent of share price fluctuations. On the other hand, the return generated from Share Price Appreciation can be affected by short-term market fluctuations up until the point when the investor sells their shares and "realizes" their gain or loss.

To further illustrate the concept of **total return**, we will use an example from an investment style similar to that of Dividend Growth Investing, namely, Real Estate Investing. *If an investor purchases a rental property for $1,000,000 today, charges their tenants $20,000 per year for rent, and after 15 years' time, the property's value appreciates to $1,400,000, what would the investor's total return be by the 15th year?* Just like Dividend Growth Investing, there are two components to the investor's total return:

1) Property Value Appreciation; and
2) Rental Income.

From the property appreciating in value, the investor would generate a $400,000 return. From the rental income, they would generate a $300,000 return. In total, the return would be $700,000; represented by the sum of both the return from property appreciation and the cash received from the rental income.

Similarly, with Dividend Growth Investing, **the total return generated by investing in a company's stock is the sum of the return from Share Price Appreciation and the return from Dividend Income.**

The following chart provides a brief summary of the components that make up "total return" for both Dividend Growth Investing and Real Estate Investing:

Investment Style	Cash Flow (Locked-In Return)	Principal Appreciation (Fluctuating Return)
Dividend Growth Investing	Dividends paid by the company directly to the investor's brokerage account on a quarterly basis.	The company's share price appreciating or depreciating in value. The return becomes "locked-in" once the investor sells his/her shares.
Real Estate Investing	Rent paid by the tenant directly to the property owner in accordance with a pre-determined payment schedule.	The property's value appreciating or depreciating in value. The return becomes "locked-in" once the property owner sells the property.

Figure A1: Components of Total Return for Dividend Growth Investing and Real Estate Investing.

As we will see in future chapters, the dividend portion of the investment represents the most important component to wealth building and achieving financial success. The regular dividend payment date represents the investor's "payday" and should generate even more excitement than receiving a pay cheque from work as the investor did not have to earn the payment by physically going to work but, instead, allowed their investment to work for them.

Dividend Growth

We are about to put the last piece of the puzzle into place, the piece that will bring together what we have discussed thus far about dividends and the role they play in Dividend Growth Investing. To explain this concept, let us return to our example of Real Estate Investing. What if instead of charging the tenants $20,000 per year in rent, the investor could increase that charge by an additional 8% on an annual basis? For example, in Year 2, the investor's rental income would be $21,600 as opposed to $20,000. The following charts compare the total return of the investment in 15 years' time with a static rent charge to that of an 8% increase in rent each year:

Static Rent:

	Year 0	Year 1	Year 5	Year 10	Year 15	Return
Property Value	$1,000,000				$1,400,000	$400,000
Rent	$0	$20,000	$20,000	$20,000	$20,000	$300,000
Total						$700,000

Figure B1: $1,000,000 property appreciating in value with static rent over a 15 year period.

Rent Growing at 8%

	Year 0	Year 1	Year 5	Year 10	Year 15	Return
Property Value	$1,000,000				$1,400,000	$400,000
Rent	$0	$20,000	$27,210	$39,980	$58,744	$543,042
Total						$943,042

Figure C1: $1,000,000 property appreciating in value with rent growing at an annual rate of eight percent over a 15 year period.

By increasing the rent by 8% each year, the investor's return generated from rental income would be 81% higher than if rent remained static. In addition, in the event that the investor requires this rental income for everyday expenditures, they can view this rental property as an indexed pension since they can rest assured knowing their income will increase at a rate faster than the rate of inflation year after year. We will continue to expand on this topic, which, in my opinion, is one of the most significant benefits of Dividend Growth Investing, in Chapter 7.

This real estate lesson truly illustrates Dividend Growth Investing's secret weapon:

*Dividend income, together with share price appreciation, can present investors with a higher return than companies that do not pay a dividend. However, **companies that continuously grow their dividends over time are the only ones that can truly maximize an investor's total return and create an indexed pension surpassing the rate of inflation.***

Long Run vs. Short Run

Unfortunately, far too many investors continue to focus their attention on picking companies that they, or the so-called financial experts, predict will generate a significant return from share price appreciation alone. To make matters worse, these investors fail to distinguish between the factors that influence a company's share price in the short run and the long run; a failure that ultimately leads to poor investment decisions. Over the next two subsections, we will discuss the following two topics:

- 1) Why focusing on the long run is essential when employing a Dividend Growth Investing approach
- 2) The positive correlation between dividend growth, earnings growth, and share price growth

Over the short run, a company's share price is influenced by factors outside of the company's control. A few of these factors include the following:

- Geopolitical factors
- Government policies
- The Media
- Investor Sentiment
- Interest Rates

Remember, even if a company is profitable, introducing new, innovative product lines, and becoming a market leader in their industry; their share price is still susceptible to downward movements over the short run since, over the short run, share prices are not influenced by a company's profitability. In other words, **over the short run, a**

company has no control over their share price. Since short run share prices are susceptible to external factors outside of a company's control, what makes investors think they can accurately predict short run share prices? The reality is that attempting to predict share prices over a short period of time for any given company is truly an exercise in futility.

With that being said, **over the long run, the gap between a company's share price and their true fundamental share value closes.** As you might imagine, the true fundamental value of any business, whether the business is publically traded or held privately, is determined by its current and future level of profitability. Since companies have control over their level of profitability, **over the long run, companies have control over the direction of their share price.**

As investors, if we are able to pinpoint companies that are likely to continue to be profitable, we can rest assured knowing their share price is bound to increase over the long run. With that being said, here comes the million dollar question: **how can we, as investors, identify companies that are likely to continue to be profitable?**

Dividends, Earnings, and Share Price – Upwards and Onwards Together

The question I posed at the end of the last subsection can be answered by viewing the interconnectivity between earnings, dividends, and share prices.

If we know that a company's fundamental value is determined by their current and future level of earnings, we know that any future share price appreciation will be contingent on the company's ability to continuously increase their earnings overtime.

As mentioned earlier in this chapter, dividends are paid from after tax dollars. For this reason, in order for a company to continuously increase their dividends paid to shareholders, they must continuously increase their earnings. Furthermore, if a company is able to continuously increase their earnings, their fundamental share value will increase since the company has increased profitability. Overtime, the market will take notice of the discrepancy between the company's fundamental share value and their share price, causing the share price to increase in order to close the gap. At this point, the bottom line should be clear:

Companies with a strong track record of continuous dividend growth must continuously grow their earnings overtime if they wish to maintain this standard of increasing their dividends paid to shareholders. As a result, their share price is likely to move upwards over the long run.

This interconnectivity between increasing corporate earnings and increasing dividends in order to increase share prices is as simple and basic as that, and has been for over 150 years.[i]

Now that you are aware of the positive correlation between earnings, dividends, and share prices, it should be quite obvious as to how investors can identify companies that are likely to continue to increase their earnings over time. **By simply seeking out companies with a strong track record of consistent dividend growth rather than speculate blindly with companies that do not pay a dividend at all, investors can identify companies that are likely to continue to increase their profitability.**

At this point, you should now have a clear understanding of the following concepts prior to carrying on with the remainder of this book:

- What is a dividend?
- The two components that make up stock market returns: 1) Share Price Appreciation, 2) Dividend Income
- The power of dividend growth
- Distinguishing between factors that influence share prices in the short run and long run
- The positive correlation between dividends, earnings, and share prices
- How investors can identify companies who are likely to continuously increase earnings by viewing their dividend track record

If you do not feel comfortable with these concepts, I encourage you to review this chapter once more prior to moving on to Chapter Two.

Additional Facts about Dividends

1. The term "DIVIDEND" derives from the Latin term "dividendum", or "thing to be divided". In other words, companies divide their profits amongst shareholders through the form of dividends.
2. Companies have been paying dividends to shareholders for over 400 years. The first company to ever pay a dividend was the Dutch East India Company in the early 1600s.
3. Historically, companies that pay dividends tend to be less volatile and have weathered down markets better than their non-dividend paying counterparts.[ii]
4. A stock's dividend yield is equal to the annual dividend payment divided by the stock's current share price. The dividend yield is expressed as a percentage and is interpreted by potential investors as the annual income they would receive for every dollar invested today. For example, if Company A's share price is $10 and they pay an annual dividend of $1 per share, the stock's current dividend yield is 10%. Furthermore, since the dividend yield is a function of the company's share price, one can expect for the dividend yield to change on a daily basis. Continuing from our last example, if

Company's A share price were to increase to $15 and their annual dividend remains fixed at $1, their dividend yield would decrease to 6.66%. In other words, a potential investor would receive $0.066 in annual income for each $1 invested today.

5. Dividends receive preferential tax treatment when compared to interest income.
6. When you own dividend growth companies, you own stakes in businesses who maintain a strong presence in their respective sectors. These tend to be profitable companies with strong business models and disciplined management.

Section Two:

The Threats to Our Financial Wealth

Chapter Two
Understated Inflation and Low Interest Rates

Let's face it: as humans, we spend most of our lives devoted to building up our financial wealth. At the age of four, we were thrown into the education system where we learned how to read, write, and solve problems. In our final year of high school, we stayed up countless nights in order to study and complete assignments, all for the sole purpose of being accepted into a prestigious college or university. Whether we pursued post-secondary education or not, at this point in our lives, we have already invested an absurd amount of time and effort into maximizing our potential for future financial wealth; yet, we likely have not earned more than the minimum wage!

Fast forward twenty years: most of us are probably working, or have worked, in an industry where all of our time and effort has finally paid off. With that being said, here comes the million dollar question: **If we spend the majority of our life striving to build our financial**

wealth, why do we not spend an equivalent amount of time trying to protect it?

Unfortunately, most Canadians forget the most important stage of the wealth management process because they are simply unaware of the many threats to their financial wealth. Over the course of Section 2, we will introduce and explain the extent to which these threats can be destructive. Later on, in Section 3, we will explain how Dividend Growth Investing provides a solution to overcome each and every one of these threats.

Understated Inflation

We have all heard the term "inflation" at some point in our lives. In simple terms, inflation is the rate at which prices for goods and services increase and, consequently, the purchasing power of our money decreases. Understanding the real inflation rate is critical in order to ensure that our investments are generating a rate of return high enough to prevent our purchasing power from eroding overtime.

To illustrate this concept, we will use an example. Let us assume the Canadian inflation rate is five percent and the annual yield provided by Investment A is three percent. Without accounting for inflation, it seems as though a potential investor would build their wealth at an annual rate of three percent if they chose to pursue this investment. However, after we take into account the effects of inflation, it quickly becomes evident that the investor's purchasing power would in fact diminish by two percent each year. In other words, the cost of goods and services in Canada increases by five percent annually but the investor's wealth grows at an annual rate of three percent, therefore, the investor's purchasing power decreases by two percent each year.

Warren Buffet, one of the world's most successful investors, once shared a wonderful visual image of inflation: "Inflation is like a mouse in our wallets, chewing away at our money in the middle of the night". Buffet's simple description illuminates what most investors tend to disregard. Put simply, when comparing different investment opportunities, we must always ensure that the rate of return is higher than the rate of inflation.

The real problem for us, as investors, is that both the government and the Bank of Canada are incentivized to maintain a relatively low rate of inflation. Of course, setting a goal for a low, stable rate is, in part, justified because it creates a stable economy, manages boom-bust cycles, creates a more competitive export market, and gives businesses greater confidence to make investments. However, the government does not speak of one additional reason because of its controversial nature. **By maintaining a low inflation rate, government payments towards those government pensions which are linked to the rate of inflation become lower.** In other words:

- **Lower Inflation = Lower Government Payments**

Since 1981, the government has changed the calculation of the inflation rate over twenty times. To make matters even more suspicious, after each change, the inflation rate has become lower. Today, the core inflation rate is made up of roughly 600 products that consumers use on an equal basis; however, many commonplace products and services such as vegetables, fruits, rent, and hydro are excluded.

According to the Fraser Institute, if the government used the same calculation of inflation as they did in 1981, which arguably provided a closer representation of real inflation, the inflation rate today would be somewhere between six and eight percent.[iii] Clearly, inflation as we know it is understated.

The following graph displays the Canadian inflation rate versus the percentage price increase for various consumer products and services from 2005-2017:

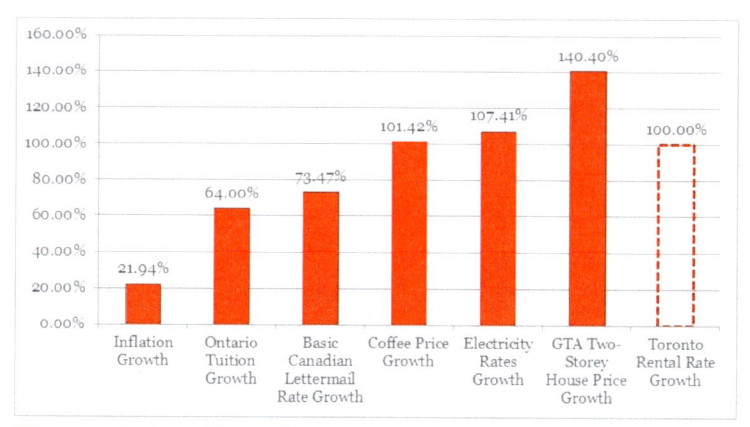

Figure A2: Canadian inflation rate versus the percentage price increase for various consumer products and services from 2005-2017.[iv]

As illustrated in *Figure A2*, the cumulative growth of Canadian inflation from 2005-2017 is substantially lower than the cumulative price increase during the same period for a few common, household products and services. Between this graph, the in-depth research conducted by the Fraser Institute, and the reality that the government may be incentivized to maintain a low rate of inflation in order to reduce their pension payments, it is safe to assume that **in order to maintain our purchasing power, we must aim**

to generate an annual average rate of return of at least six percent.

Low Interest Rates

Now that we understand that the real inflation rate is somewhere between six and eight percent, the solution seems pretty straightforward: invest in securities that will generate an annual average return of at least six to eight percent. Now ask yourself, does this return sound attainable from a guaranteed investment certificate (GIC) from your local bank? In fact, when was the last time GIC rates were even remotely close to six percent?

In recent times, GICs have provided investors with an annual average return of roughly two percent. I generally refer to GICs as "GLCs", also known as "Guaranteed Loss Certificates", because the only "guarantee" is that investors are "guaranteed" to lose their purchasing power year after year.

To further emphasize just how detrimental the combination of understated inflation and a low interest rate environment is, let us use an example of a sixty-year-old, newly retired woman who would like her portfolio to provide her with a level of income that is sufficient to be able to live comfortably for the entirety of her retirement years. She decides to visit her local branch and provides her advisor with the following pieces of information:

    1) I have $1,000,000 saved.

    2) I believe I will live up until the age of 90.

    3) I am an extremely conservative investor.

In our previous example, most novice advisors would make the detrimental mistake of advising that the most suitable investment for an "extremely conservative" investor is one with extremely low volatility. As a result, they may proceed to recommend for the client to invest the $1,000,000 into a GIC yielding an annual average rate of return of two percent, an investment that the industry considers to be "extremely conservative".[1] The following graph provides an illustration of the client's purchasing power over the remainder of her life, assuming she lives up until the age of 90 and that her $1,000,000 portfolio is able to generate a rate of return of two percent. Also, we will assume the real rate of inflation is eight percent:

---

[1] As of the time of writing, prevailing Canadian market rates for one-year annual GICs are roughly 2%.

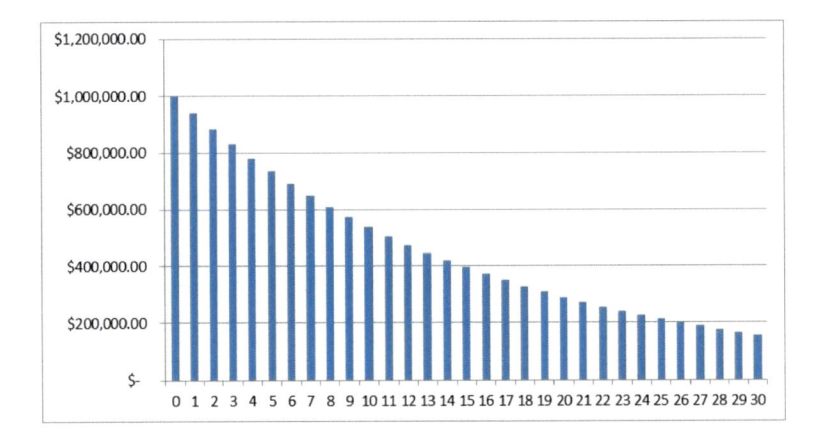

[Bar chart showing portfolio value declining from $1,000,000 at year 0 to approximately $175,000 at year 30]

Figure B2: Purchasing Power of $1,000,000 portfolio growing at two percent annually with real inflation at eight percent.

As shown, after just 11 years, the investor's purchasing power would have diminished by an astounding 50%.

As seen in our example, this type of recommendation to invest in an "extremely conservative" security, a GIC, is in fact extremely risky. Even though the client's original principal of $1,000,000 is guaranteed, the downside is that her return will most likely not be sufficient enough to keep up with the real rate of inflation. Since the client's return is fixed at two percent but the real rate of inflation is eight percent, her purchasing power would diminish year after year at a rate of six percent.

Understanding that the client's risk tolerance is dependent on the length of time she has available to remain invested rather than her perceived risk tolerance is a fundamental element to portfolio management. It is the advisor's responsibility to educate clients of the notion that **short-term market fluctuations are the price investors pay to generate premium returns in the long run**. With a long-term time horizon, an investor's portfolio has more time to recover from short-term market fluctuations whereas with a short-term time horizon, an investor may require the funds to be liquidated at a point in time when the market is in a state of recovery. We will expand on the topic of "How to optimally choose securities" in future chapters.

As demonstrated through the previous example, even though the two percent return seemed adequate on its own, it quickly became apparent that, once real inflation was factored in, a two percent return should be perceived as a six percent loss of purchasing power. Since the client specified that she has a 30-year investment period, the optimal investment decision would have been to invest in more volatile securities with the potential for above average returns.

When you consider the issues regarding personal finance that keep you up at night, have understated inflation and low interest rates ever been a factor? I am going to go out on a limb and assume that most people have never taken these threats into account but, instead, have been more concerned with other, more common factors, such as their salary, expenses, and the volatility of their portfolio. I am not trying to suggest that these factors are not important, but rather, I would simply like to present you with this inconvenient truth:

Before you go to bed at night, just remember that for every day your money is invested in a GIC, Buffet's mouse is secretly eating away at your wealth.

Chapter Three

Longevity Risk

Every day, we put more and more principles into practice that will hopefully allow us to live a long and healthy life. We are told to eat natural foods, exercise regularly, stay away from smoking; the list is endless.

In addition to society's emphasis on adopting a healthy and active lifestyle, innovation in the medical field is also growing at an incredible rate. On October 26th, 2016, a panel of top doctors and researchers at Cleveland Clinic unveiled their Top 10 Medical Innovations expected to transform healthcare in the near future. Included in the list were such breakthroughs as smart cars that reduce accidents and injuries, immunotherapy that helps children beat cancer without chemotherapy, and even stent cells that harmlessly dissolve after their work is complete.[v] These ongoing advancements in the medical world, coupled with a greater commitment to a healthy lifestyle, have led to **a significant increase in the average lifespan of human beings year after year.**

Without a doubt, the fact that people are living longer is generally regarded as a positive. However, there is a risk associated with living longer, a risk directly targeting our hard-earned financial wealth and lifestyle in retirement. **Longevity Risk**, the risk of running out of money during our retirement years, is one of the most detrimental threats to our financial wealth which has been overlooked for far too long by the investment community.

Longevity Risk

The following graph illustrates the trend toward increasing life expectancy in Canada from 1901 to 2016:

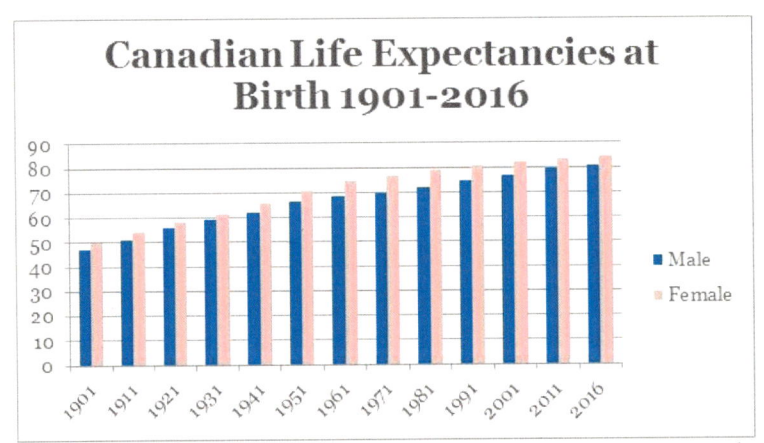

Figure A3: Canadian life expectancy at birth from 1901 to 2016.[vi]

When we factor in how long the human race has walked the face of this earth, the notion that Canadian life expectancy has increased by roughly 68 percent in only 100 years is absolutely astounding. The reality is that this trend will not only continue, but is likely to increase at a faster rate as time progresses.

What does this mean for Canadians? Well, simply put, if we live for a longer period of time while holding our retirement age fixed at 65, our years spent in retirement will increase. Living longer during a period of our lives with no income suggests that we must have more money available on the first day of retirement to survive comfortably for the remainder of our years.

To illustrate just how significant the impact of increased life expectancy is from a financial planning perspective, let us compare the amount of money required on the first day of retirement for a 65 year old male in 1981 to a 65 year old male in 2016. For the sake of simplicity, we will make the following assumptions:

- Both individuals require $100,000 per year to live comfortably in retirement.
- The rate of inflation is constant.
- Both individuals' portfolios in retirement generate an annual average return of 4%.

- Payments are withdrawn on the first day of the year; therefore, the return is generated on the "after-withdrawn portfolio value" of the coinciding year.
- *Portfolio Value* represents the value of the individual's portfolio as of the last day of their current birth year. For example, a $454,595 portfolio for an individual aged 66 represents the portfolio value on the last day that they are 66 years old, or in other words, the day before their 67th birthday.
- *Withdrawal* is the amount withdrawn from the individual's portfolio on the first day of their current birth year. For example, an individual who withdrew $100,000 at age 66 represents a withdrawal on the first day that they turned 66 years old, or in other words, their 66th birthday.
- Each individual passes away on the birthday of the year coinciding with the average lifespan of their demographic group.
- The average lifespan of a Canadian male in 1981 is 72.
- The average lifespan of a Canadian male in 2016 is 80.

65 Year Old Canadian Male Retiree in 1981

Age	64	65	66	67	68
Portfolio Value (EOY)	**$607,569**	$532,947	$454,595	$372,324	$285,941
Withdrawal (BOY)	N/A	$100,000	$100,000	$100,000	$100,000

Age	69	70	71
Portfolio Value (EOY)	$195,238	$100,000	$0.00
Withdrawal (BOY)	$100,000	$100,000	$100,000

Figure B3: Portfolio value over retirement years of 65 year old Canadian Male Retiree who begins retirement in 1981.

65 Year Old Canadian Male Retiree in 2016

Age	64	65	66	67	68
Portfolio Value (EOY)	**$1,089,864**	$1,039,357	$986,325	$930,641	$872,173
Withdrawal (BOY)	N/A	$100,000	$100,000	$100,000	$100,000

Age	69	70	71	72	73
Portfolio Value (EOY)	$810,782	$746,321	$678,637	$607,569	$532,948
Withdrawal (BOY)	$100,000	$100,000	$100,000	$100,000	$100,000

Age	74	75	76	77	78	79
Portfolio Value (EOY)	$454,595	$372,325	$285,941	$195,238	$100,000	$0
Withdrawal (BOY)	$100,000	$100,000	$100,000	$100,000	$100,000	$100,000

Figure C3: Portfolio value over retirement years of 65 year old Canadian Male Retiree who begins retirement in 2016.

Under this basic example, **the average Canadian male retiree in 2016 must save an additional 79%, or $482,295, more than the average Canadian male retiree in 1981 by their final year of employment in order to live comfortably for the remainder of their retirement years**. This realization truly emphasizes the importance of taking a proactive approach with regards to beginning the retirement planning process as soon as possible.

Now that we understand the significant threat Longevity Risk poses to our financial wealth, let us take a look at the three broad solutions available to Canadians:

1) Save more money during their working years.
2) Work beyond the traditional retirement age of 65.
3) Invest in securities with a higher expected rate of return.

While the first point regarding "savings" is extremely important, the focus of this book remains on the topic of investing. Moreover, while working beyond the traditional age of 65 is definitely possible, and unfortunately necessary for many Canadians, we believe there is a more efficient approach, one that does not involve putting unnecessary stress on our body at a time when we are expected to wind down and relax. By process of elimination, the following two subsections will focus on: 1) How society's flawed view of "risk" has prevented investors from choosing securities that will generate a relatively high expected return, and 2) How we can convert the risk associated with longevity to a positive through the Power of Compounding Interest.

Longevity Risk vs. Society's View of Risk

. Unfortunately, society associates the concept of "portfolio risk" with the ***probability that their portfolio's returns will fluctuate in the short run***. This false notion has driven many Canadians to believe that they should simply search for investment opportunities with extremely low risk, or, in simpler terms, extremely low volatility.

The investment elites have encouraged this false notion by stating **"risk"** as the **"volatility of returns of a specific investment security"**. In the investment world, this means that the larger the difference between the returns of a single investment year after year, the higher level of risk associated with that specific investment.

Naturally, individuals who consider themselves to be "risk averse" end up investing in securities which will minimize their volatility. In Chapter Two, we provided an example which illustrated this exact situation:

- A 60 year old, newly retired, woman with $1,000,000 saved. This woman believes she will live up until the age of 90 and considers herself to be an extremely conservative investor.
- The advisor provides a recommendation to construct a portfolio comprised of 100% GICs, completely eliminating all volatility within the portfolio. The advisor's reasoning to back up this recommendation was to limit the client's exposure to volatility since the client considers herself to be "extremely conservative".

Under the terms of a traditional GIC, the investor invests a fixed amount on Day 1, earns fixed annual interest payments over the term of the investment period, and at the end of the term, the principal is returned to the investor. Over the entire investment period, the individual's return is fixed and principal is guaranteed; therefore, the security has zero volatility.

While the advisor's recommendation in our example coincides with society's perception of risk (lower risk tolerance = construct a lower volatility portfolio), it can still be quite risky. To illustrate why society's understanding of risk is extremely flawed and, in fact, impedes our ability to build a large enough portfolio to last the entirety of our retirement years, we will compare the returns of two separate investments:

- **Investment A (Volatile)** posted returns of 10% in Year 1, -5% in Year 2, and 16% in Year 3, representing an annual average return of 7%;
- **Investment B (GIC)** posted returns of 2% in each of Years 1, 2, and 3, representing an annual average return of 2%.

Notice how the annual returns of **Investment B** have been fixed at 2% each year while the returns of **Investment A** have been volatile? In fact, Investment A actually earned a negative return in its second year. Despite its volatile nature, Investment A actually generated a significantly higher annual average return over a three-year period than Investment B. Arguably the most important concept that the investment community fails to grasp is that in the long run, volatile investments have historically outperformed investments with a fixed rate of return.

Over the long run, premium returns are rewarded to those who have the fortitude to withstand the emotional stress associated with volatile returns and temporary declines in their portfolio's value. These short-term market fluctuations are simply the price investors pay for premium returns in the long run. **As for investors who choose to construct a portfolio with minimum volatility, the price they pay for the benefit of eliminating the emotional stress associated with volatile returns and temporary declines in their portfolio's value is lower returns over long periods of time.**

The following chart provides a general summary of the concepts explained:

Higher Volatility	Lower Volatility
Higher long-term returns	Lower long-terms returns
More emotional stress	Less emotional stress
Suitable for investors with long time horizons	Suitable for investors with short time horizons

Figure D3: Average characteristics of higher volatility investment versus lower volatility investment.

The natural response to our example which compares Investment A and Investment B is that it is, in fact, just an example. To provide actual, concrete evidence to support our example, let us compare the five year annual average return of the S&P/TSX Composite Index, an index which tracks the performance of the Canadian stock market, to the rate quoted for the average five year GIC provided by any of the major Canadian financial institutions roughly five years prior to writing.

- Annual Average Five-Year Total Return of S&P/TSX Composite Index = **8.90%**[2]
- Five-Year GIC Rate Provided by Tangerine = **2.25%**[3,vii]

---

[2] June 30th, 2013 to June 30th, 2018
[3] Offered as of July 5th, 2012

Over the past five years, Canadian investors who had the ability to withstand the short-term market fluctuations associated with the stock market would have generated an annual average return significantly higher than that generated from the average five year GIC.

The concept of viewing risk as the probability that your portfolio will temporarily drop in value in the short run is the most detrimental threat to wealth creation. This notion encourages people to invest in extremely low volatile investments such as GICs, and consequently, earn extremely low returns. The false societal perception of risk negatively affects our ability to defend ourselves against the real threat, **longevity risk**. By investing in low volatile securities, we are guaranteeing low, long-term returns and increasing the risk that we will not save enough money for retirement.

The Power of Compounding Interest

At this point, you should have a clear understanding of the following:

1) The significant impact a longer retirement period has on our financial planning requirements.

2) Society's flawed view of "risk" motivates investors to believe "low risk" = "low volatility" which, in turn, makes their ability to generate a return sufficient enough to reach the point where they have enough money to last the entirety of their retirement years even more difficult.

In this last subsection, I would like to provide an introduction to an investment tool that transforms "Longevity" from a threat to our financial wealth to a supplement; **The Power of Compounding Interest**. To explain this concept, we will first provide definitions for both Simple Interest and Compound Interest:

- **Simple Interest**: The percentage return generated by a security is based off the investor's original principal.
- **Compound Interest**: The percentage return generated by a security is based off the investor's original principal plus all previously generated returns.

As you can see, there is one small, yet powerful, difference between Simple Interest and Compound Interest: returns generated by compound interest enabled securities compound on all of the wealth accumulated through previous returns in addition to the original principal.

We will illustrate the power of this tool by comparing the dollar returns of a simple interest yielding security to a compound interest yielding security.

Security A – Simple Interest

- $100,000 invested in a 5.6% yielding GIC.
- The infamous GIC is considered a Simple Interest yielding security because the annual interest payments are based solely off the original principal invested.

Security B – Compound Interest

- $100,000 invested in the Canadian stock market yielding an annual average return of 5.6%.
- The stock market is notorious for being one of the most efficient methods for utilizing the power of compound interest. Consider an investor who holds $100,000 of Stock A. Over a 3-day period, the daily returns are as follows:
    - Day 1: 0.5%
    - Day 2: -1.0%
    - Day 3: 1.5%

- After the first day, the investor's portfolio is valued at $100,500. On the second day, the -1.0% return is generated off the $100,500 rather than the original $100,000. Therefore, after Day 2, the investor's portfolio is valued at $99,495. After Day 3, the investor generates a 1.5% return off the $99,495, bringing the portfolio value up to $100,985.
- Since stock market returns are based off the original principal plus all previously generated returns, stocks are considered compound interest securities.

Note: The 5.6% return used in this example was not chosen at random. Instead, it coincides with the annual average return of the Canadian stock market since the year 1900.

The following chart represents the growth of both Security A and Security B over the course of a 50-year period:

Year	Security A	Security B
0	$100,000.00	$100,000.00
1	$105,600.00	$105,600.00
2	$111,200.00	$111,513.60
3	$116,800.00	$117,758.36
4	$122,400.00	$124,352.83
5	$128,000.00	$131,316.59
6	$133,600.00	$138,670.32
7	$139,200.00	$146,435.86
8	$144,800.00	$154,636.26
9	$150,400.00	$163,295.89
10	$156,000.00	$172,440.46
11	$161,600.00	$182,097.13
12	$167,200.00	$192,294.57
13	$172,800.00	$203,063.06
14	$178,400.00	$214,434.60
15	$184,000.00	$226,442.93
16	$189,600.00	$239,123.74
17	$195,200.00	$252,514.67
18	$200,800.00	$266,655.49
19	$206,400.00	$281,588.20
20	$212,000.00	$297,357.14
21	$217,600.00	$314,009.13
22	$223,200.00	$331,593.65
23	$228,800.00	$350,162.89
24	$234,400.00	$369,772.01
25	$240,000.00	$390,479.25
26	$245,600.00	$412,346.08

27	$251,200.00	$435,437.46
28	$256,800.00	$459,821.96
29	$262,400.00	$485,571.99
30	$268,000.00	$512,764.02
31	$273,600.00	$541,478.81
32	$279,200.00	$571,801.62
33	$284,800.00	$603,822.51
34	$290,400.00	$637,636.57
35	$296,000.00	$673,344.22
36	$301,600.00	$711,051.50
37	$307,200.00	$750,870.38
38	$312,800.00	$792,919.12
39	$318,400.00	$837,322.59
40	$324,000.00	$884,212.66
41	$329,600.00	$933,728.57
42	$335,200.00	$986,017.37
43	$340,800.00	$1,041,234.34
44	$346,400.00	$1,099,543.46
45	$352,000.00	$1,161,117.90
46	$357,600.00	$1,226,140.50
47	$363,200.00	$1,294,804.37
48	$368,800.00	$1,367,313.41
49	$374,400.00	$1,443,882.96
50	$380,000.00	$1,524,740.41

Figure E3: Growth of Security A and Security B over the course of a 50-year period.

After 50 years, the 5.6% annual compounded return provided by the Canadian stock market generated an astounding $1,144,740.41 more than the 5.6% annual simple return provided by the GIC. In percentage terms, the stock market generated a 1425% return whereas the GIC generated a relatively pathetic 280% return.

At this point, you may be asking yourself the following question:

How can two securities offering the same annual average rates of return generate extremely different returns in dollar terms?

To address this question, we will take a closer look at the previous chart using the knowledge we have obtained over the course of this chapter. Specifically, we will compare the annual return in dollar terms for the following three years:

    1) The annual return in the first year, Year 1.
    2) The annual return in Year 10.
    3) The annual return in the final year, Year 50.

Over Year 1, both Security A, the GIC, and Security B, the Canadian stock market, generated a dollar return of $5,600. Security A's 5.6% simple return was generated solely off the original principal, equating to a dollar return of $5,600. Security B's 5.6% compounded return was generated off the original principal, plus all previously generated returns. However, since this was the first investment year and, therefore, there are no prior returns to be compounded; Security B's dollar return in Year 1 comes out to $5,600. **Year 1 is the only year where Security A and Security B generate identical returns because there are no previously generated returns from which Security B can compound off of.**

Over Year 10, Security A generated a dollar return of $5,600, while Security B generated a dollar return of $9,144.57. Once again, Security A's 5.6% simple return was generated solely off the original principal, equating to a dollar return of $5,600. On the other hand, Security B's 5.6% compounded return was generated off the original principal, plus all returns generated from the previous nine years, equating to a $9,144.57 dollar return. **After only 10 years, the annual dollar return provided by Security B is 63% higher than the annual dollar return provided by Security A.**

To truly emphasize the incredible power of compound interest, we will now compare the annual dollar return generated by Security A to that of Security B for the final investment year. Over Year 50, Security A generated a 5.6% simple return solely off the original principal, equating to a dollar return of $5,600. In another universe altogether, Security B generated a 5.6% compounded return off the original principal, plus all previous returns generated over the prior 49 years. As a result, Security B generated a dollar return of $80,857.45. **After 50 years, the annual dollar return provided by Security B is 1344% higher than the annual dollar return provided by Security A.**

The following graph illustrates the growth of both securities over the 50-year period. Besides the fact that Security B ultimately generates a return significantly higher than that of Security A, a more important takeaway lies in the illustration which follows. As you can see, Security B's value goes up at an increasing rate whereas Security A's value increases at a fixed rate. **Since compounded interest results in a higher dollar return year after year, the longer an investor leaves their investment to compound, the more powerful it becomes.**

[Chart showing Security A and Security B growth over 50 years, with Security B reaching $1,524,740.41 and Security A reaching $380,000.00]

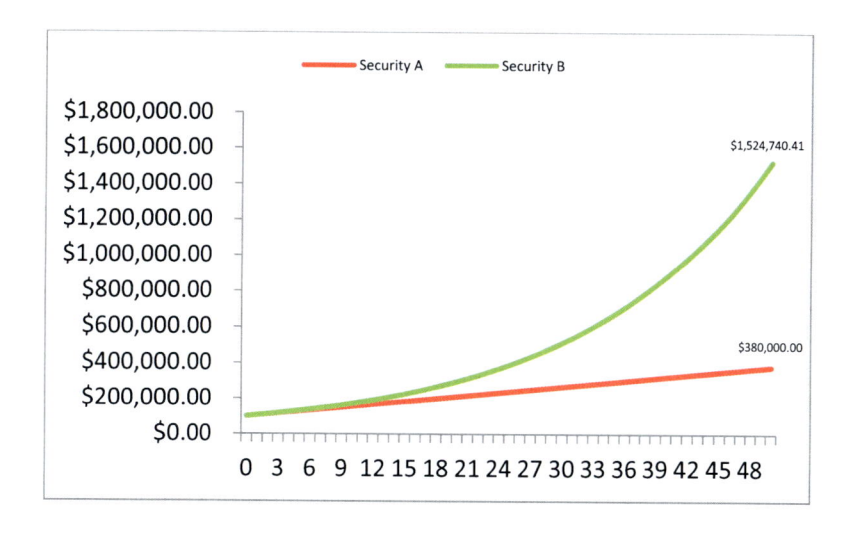

Figure F3: Growth of Security A and Security B over the course of a 50-year period.

The final takeaway from this subsection should be straightforward: **The longer the time period a compound interest security has to compound, the larger the annual dollar returns will become.**

Investors who choose to disregard the notion that volatile securities should automatically be considered "high risk" will truly be able to take advantage of compound interest. In doing so, the true risk to their financial wealth, not saving enough money to last for the entirety of their retirement years, will be minimized.

We have finally discussed "the trifecta" of outliving our retirement money: **understated inflation**, **low interest**

rates, and **longevity risk**. Over the rest of this section, we will examine two more detrimental threats to our financial wealth at which point my readers will be fully equipped with the knowledge to understand why the need for a solution is so urgent.

Chapter Four:
Taxes

I will never forget the look on my daughter's face the day she received her first pay cheque. A few summers ago, her track and field club hired her as a junior counsellor, promising her an hourly wage of $20. Before she had even started, she began to calculate the amount of her first pay cheque. Assuming a fifteen-hour work week, she figured that she would receive $600 every two weeks - not bad for a first job.

Fast forward two weeks and the day she had been looking forward to had finally arrived - pay day. I dropped her off at the track and field club, ran a few errands, and returned to pick her up later in the day with the expectation that she would be in a great mood. Was I ever wrong. The instant she hopped into the car she complained about what she considered to be an error with her pay. She was certain that she should have received $600 but her pay cheque was only in the amount of $495.

On this day, my daughter learned two valuable lessons:

1) For any economic activity, whether it be consumption, earnings, investment income or capital gains, the government will take a piece of the pie; and

2) If someone promises to pay a 16-year old $20/hour tax-free, you better believe that it is too good to be true.

From an investment management perspective, taxes are one of the greatest threats to our financial wealth. Unfortunately, most people live day-by-day conforming to the idea that they have no control over the taxes they pay.

Over the course of this chapter, we will:

- Explain the nature of how taxes are charged on equity and fixed income returns.
- Illustrate the extent to which taxes can limit our ability to save enough money to last the entirety of our retirement years.
- Provide solutions for how we, as investors, can limit our tax liability.

The Nature of What is Taxed

Before we discuss the impact of taxes on our financial

wealth, it is important to understand how these taxes are charged. Despite the endless means by which the Canadian government taxes its citizens, we will focus on three tax outlets that have the most significant impact on investment returns: 1) Taxes on Interest Income, 2) Taxes on Dividend Income, and 3) Taxes on Capital Gains. For all three channels, we will provide an example to compare the differences of each tax structure and the ultimate impact on the investor's return.

Interest Income:

Interest income, the income received from a fixed income security, is taxed at the investor's marginal tax rate without any preferential tax treatment. Since interest income is taxable in the year it is received and investors have no control over the year the income is paid, they have no control over when they will pay their tax liability. In other words, when an investor receives interest, they are immediately liable for the associated taxes.

For example, assume an Ontarian investor owns a $1,000,000 corporate bond paying semi-annual coupon payments of two percent. Since the investor's 2018 gross employment income amounted to $150,000, her combined federal and provincial marginal tax rate is 47.97%[viii]. Over the course of one year, the investor would receive $40,000 in gross interest payments. As a result, she would incur a tax liability of $19,188 since interest income is charged at the investor's marginal tax rate without any preferential tax treatment. After all is said and done, the investor's net return would be $20,812. Since the investor had no control over the interest payment schedule, she had no control over the timing of her tax liability.

Dividend Income:

Similar to interest income, dividend investors are limited in their ability to control the timing of their tax liability because they cannot control the time at which the dividends are paid. Instead, the company's board of directors agree on a dividend payout schedule and the investor's tax liability is incurred on the same day the dividend payment is made.

While both dividend- and interest-seeking investors do not have any control over the timing of their tax liability, the magnitude of the tax charged on dividend income is lower than that charged on interest income as a result of preferential tax treatment for shareholders in dividend paying companies. This preferential tax treatment is an initiative by the government to motivate investment in Canadian companies. In addition, since companies pay dividends from after-tax profits, in other words, the dividends have already been taxed at the corporate level, preferential tax treatment for shareholders in dividend paying companies aims to eliminate double taxation.

This preferential tax treatment for dividend income is provided through the **Dividend Gross-up and Tax Credit Mechanism**. The following example provides an illustration as to how this mechanism is carried out:

Assume the same investor from our previous example decides to invest $1,000,000 in a publically traded Canadian company paying an annual dividend of four percent, instead of purchasing the corporate bond. Since the investor's 2018 gross income amounted to $150,000, her combined federal and provincial marginal tax rate is 47.97%. As we will show through our next example, once the Dividend Gross-up and Tax Credit Mechanism is put into effect, the investor's effective tax rate for Canadian eligible dividends will amount to 31.67%[ix], significantly lower than what would be taxed had she invested in the $1,000,000 corporate bond. In the text which follows, I have provided a step by step breakdown of how the gross up, dividend tax, and dividend tax credit are applied:

1) The investor receives four gross dividend payments amounting to a total of $40,000.

2) On the investor's tax return, her $40,000 in dividends is "grossed up" by 38%[4][x] to $55,200. The "gross up" represents a return of the taxes that were previously charged at the corporate level. This "gross up" is applied in an attempt to eliminate double taxation.

3) Now that the total dividends are free from tax at the corporate level, the investor's marginal tax rate of 47.97% is applied to the total "grossed up" dividends. As a result, the gross tax liability is calculated to be $26,479.44.

4) The combined Federal and Provincial (Ontario) dividend tax credit in 2018 is 25.02%[xi] of the "grossed up" dividends. In our example, the dividend tax credit is calculated to be $13,811.04. After the tax credit is applied, the investor's net tax liability is calculated to

---

[4] 2018 dividend gross up percentage in Ontario

be $12,668.40. **The $12,668.40 tax liability is equivalent to a 31.67% effective tax rate for Canadian eligible dividends.**

As we have seen through the previous example, while interest-seeking investors and dividend-seeking investors may have the same level of control over the timing of their tax liability, preferential tax treatment is provided to those who invest in dividend paying stocks over fixed income securities.

Capital Gains:

The tax paid on capital gains differs from that paid on interest and dividend income because investors have the ability to control when they will pay their tax liability. Investors have this control because taxes on capital gains are only triggered when an investor sells their security and "realizes" their gain or loss. Prior to this point, the gain or loss is considered to be "unrealized" since the security still has the potential to fluctuate in value. In addition to being able to control the timing of their tax liability, investors also have the ability to use capital losses to offset their capital gains and lower their overall tax liability. We will illustrate how capital gains taxes are charged in Canada through the following example:

In Canada, 50% of capital gains are taxed at the investor's marginal tax rate. In this example, we will assume the same investor from our previous two examples decides to purchase $500,000 of Stock A and $500,000 of Stock B instead of purchasing the corporate bond or Canadian dividend paying company. It is important to note that both Stock A and Stock B do not pay a dividend. Over one year, Stock A increases in value by $80,000 and Stock B decreases in value by $40,000, representing a combined, unrealized capital gain of $40,000. At the end of the year, the investor decides to sell both Stock A and Stock B, realizing her combined gain of $40,000. As mentioned in our previous examples, since the investor's 2018 gross income amounted to $150,000, her combined federal and provincial marginal tax rate is 47.97%. The following step-by step list summarizes the nature of how the tax liability would be charged and how the investor uses the capital loss from Stock B to lower her overall tax liability:

1) Despite the fact that the investor generated an $80,000 capital gain off the sale of Stock A, she can use the $40,000 loss from Stock B to lower the total capital

gains subject to taxes. Therefore, rather than being taxed individually on the $80,000 capital gain from Stock A, the investor is taxed off the $40,000 combined capital gain from both Stock A and Stock B.

- **Extra Note**: Capital losses that have not been used to reduce a tax liability in prior years can be brought forward and used to reduce a tax liability in the current year.

2) As mentioned, in Canada, 50% of capital gains are taxed at the investor's marginal tax rate. Since 50% of the investor's combined capital gain amounts to $20,000, only $20,000 is subject to being taxed at the investor's marginal tax rate. As a result, the investor's total tax liability amounts to $9,594.

From the previous example, not only did the investor have control over the timing of her tax liability, the magnitude of her tax liability was also lower than the taxes charged on interest income and dividend income. In fact, at a marginal tax rate of 47.97%, her effective tax rate for capital gains was only 23.98%. The following chart summarizes the characteristics of the tax liability for interest income, dividend income, and capital gains:

	Interest Income	**Dividend Income**	**Capital Gains**
Tax Liability Control	Subject to the interest payment schedule chosen by the issuing institution. The investor has zero control.	Subject to the dividend payment schedule chosen by the company's board of directors. The investor has zero control.	Subject to the point at which the investor decides to sell his or her securities. The investor has complete control.
Magnitude of Tax Liability	Taxed at the investor's marginal tax rate with no preferential tax treatment. This form of taxation results in the highest tax liability.	Taxed at the investor's marginal tax rate with preferential tax treatment. The investor receives a dividend tax credit to reduce their overall tax liability. This form of taxation results in a lower tax liability than interest income, but higher tax liability than capital gains.	50% of the investor's capital gains is taxed at the investor's marginal tax rate. This form of taxation results in the lowest tax liability.

Figure A4: Characteristics of tax liabilities for interest income, dividend income, and capital gains.

How Taxes Destroy Long-Term Performance

As previously mentioned, taxes are one of the most detrimental threats to reaching our long-term investment objectives. To illustrate this point, we will take a look at an example where an investor holds a portfolio of only fixed income securities. For simplicity, let us make the following assumptions:

- The investor will invest $1,000,000 for 25 years.
- The portfolio will earn an annual return of three percent. For simplicity, we will assume that the investment pays interest income once per year and the investor chooses to reinvest the proceeds into the same investment.
- The investor's marginal tax rate will be fixed at 45%.

The following figure compares the return of his portfolio after a 25-year period with and without taxes:

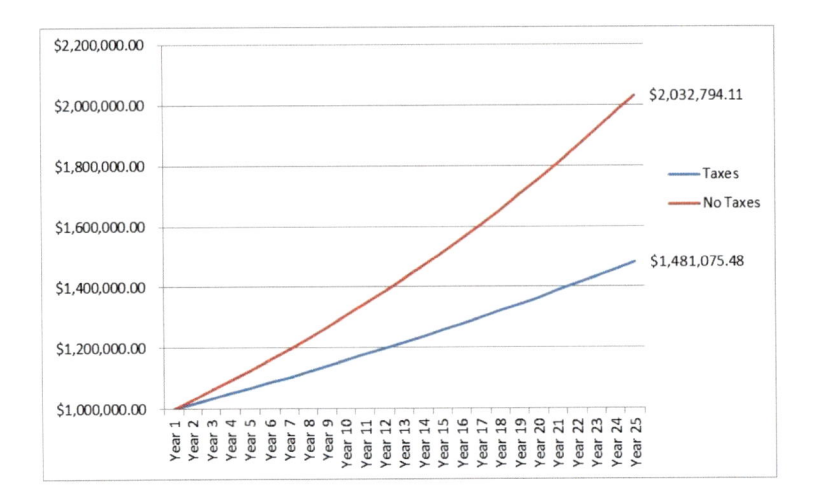

Figure B4: Growth of an investor's portfolio over 25-years with and without taxes.

As you can see, the taxes actually limit the investor's return by significantly more than his 45% marginal tax rate. **In fact, without taxes, the investor's initial investment of $1,000,000 was able to grow 55% more, or $551,718.63 more, than the investment with taxes.** If both investments are identical, other than the fact that one incurs an annual tax liability of 45% and the other does not, how can the difference in returns exceed 45%?

Put simply, when an investor reinvests the proceeds from his or her original investment, his investment will now earn a higher dollar return in the following year because the interest is compounding on a higher amount. For example, in the first year of the investment period without taxes, the investor earned $30,000, or in percentage terms, three percent. In the second year, he earned an additional three percent, however, this time the three percent was generated off the original principal plus the return generated in the previous year. Therefore, the three percent return in the second year was actually generated off of $1,030,000, amounting to an annual return of $30,900. Since the investment with taxes compounds off a smaller amount of previously generated returns year after year, the investment with taxes increases at a slower rate than the investment without taxes.

Using the knowledge obtained from previous chapters, can you remember the name of the investment tool responsible for the 55% difference in returns from the previous example? If you guessed **Compound Interest**, you have been paying attention. Since taxes on investment income continually reduce the investor's return throughout the investment period, the total dollar amount from which all prior year returns can be compounded is reduced.

To summarize, **taxes are detrimental to our financial wealth because they limit our ability to make use of the Power of Compounding Interest.**

It is important to realize that taxes had a significant impact in our previous example because the investment return was made up of strictly interest income; therefore, the investor was taxed at their marginal tax rate with no preferential tax treatment. To make matters worse, the investor also had no control over the timing of his tax liability.

In the final subsection of this chapter, we will explain how Canadians can reduce their overall tax liability from interest income, dividend income, and capital gains by optimally allocating certain asset classes to be held within specific investment accounts. This strategy is also referred to as **Asset Location**.

Asset Location

In Canada, investors can hold their investment securities within a number of different investment accounts. A few of these accounts offer unique tax-sheltered and tax-free benefits, providing investors with a platform to optimally allocate asset classes to the account type that will minimize their overall tax liability. In this subsection, we will explain how investors can reduce their overall tax liability through making proper use of the following three account types:

- 1) Non-Registered
- 2) Registered Retirement Savings Plan (RRSP)
- 3) Tax-Free Savings Plan (TFSA)

It is important to note that these three accounts happen to be the most common account types in Canada. In reality, there are a number of additional account types that offer more specific, yet, similar tax reduction benefits.

Non-Registered

A non-registered account is the most standard, basic account offered to Canadians. The account offers no tax benefits and imposes no restrictions on contributions or withdrawals.

Registered Retirement Savings Plan (RRSP)

A registered retirement savings plan shelters all securities within the account from taxation until the investor decides to withdraw funds from the account. In other words, regardless of whether an interest payment is made, dividend payment is made, or the investor chooses to sell their securities and realize a capital gain, no tax liability is applied. If the investor chooses to make a withdrawal, the funds withdrawn are taxed at the investor's marginal tax rate. The three main benefits of an RRSP are as follows:

1) The individual tax laws for each asset class is eliminated. In other words, regardless of whether the security generates an interest return, dividend return, or capital gains return, the tax liability is calculated by multiplying the investor's withdrawal amount by his or her marginal tax rate.

2) Since a tax liability only applies if the investor decides to withdraw funds from his or her account, investment returns are able to compound tax-free. Once again, all investment returns will not be taxed. Only at the point in which the investor chooses to make a withdrawal will the amount withdrawn be taxed at the investor's marginal tax rate.

3) An RRSP provides investors with complete control over the timing of their tax liability. As we now know, investors of interest and dividend paying securities have no control over the timing of their tax liability if the securities are held in a non-registered account. However, since the RRSP creates a unified tax system

for all asset classes, a tax liability only applies once the investor decides to withdraw funds from the account.

In addition to the benefits previously listed, Canadians are able to lower their taxable income by making contributions to their RRSP. With that being said, we do not consider this to be a benefit from an investment management perspective, therefore, it has not been included in the previous list.

With respect to restrictions, Canadians are limited in the annual amount they can contribute to their RRSP. This amount depends on multiple parameters that are specific to the investor, therefore, we will not be covering this topic in our book.

Tax-Free Savings Account (TFSA)

While an RRSP offers tax-sheltered benefits, the tax-free savings account completely eliminates taxes associated with interest income, dividend income, and capital gains altogether. In addition, any amounts that the investor withdraws from their account are not taxed and can even be re-contributed to the same account in the following calendar year. The main drawback with the TFSA is that the contribution room is extremely low relative to that of a non-registered or RRSP. The following chart lists both the annual and cumulative TFSA contribution room provided for an individual that was at least 18 years of age in 2009, the first year the TFSA came into effect:

Year	Annual Contribution Limit	Cumulative Contribution Limit
2009	$5,000	$5,000
2010	$5,000	$10,000
2011	$5,000	$15,000
2012	$5,000	$20,000
2013	$5,500	$25,500
2014	$5,500	$31,000
2015	$10,000	$41,000
2016	$5,500	$46,500
2017	$5,500	$52,000
2018	$5,500	$57,500

Figure C4: Annual and cumulative TFSA contribution room provided for an individual that was at least 18 years of age in 2009, the first year the TFSA came into effect.[xii]

It is important to take note of the cumulative contribution limit in addition to the annual contribution limit since investors who missed contributions in previous years are able to make these contributions in the current year. For example, if a 50-year-old investor opened a TFSA in 2018 for the very first time, they would be able to contribute the full $57,500.

Now that we have an understanding of the benefits and limitations associated with each account type, we can take a look at how investors can reduce their overall investment tax liability by properly allocating securities among these accounts.

Interest Paying Fixed Income Securities

Earlier in this chapter, we provided three examples of a single investor who generates a $40,000 return in the form of interest income, dividend income, and capital gains. The results proved that interest income is associated with the largest tax burden for the following reasons:

1) Investors are taxed at their marginal tax rate with no preferential tax treatment.
2) Investors have no control over the timing of their tax liability.

For these reasons, to minimize an investor's overall investment tax liability I believe the investor's first priority should be to hold interest-paying securities within an RRSP.[5] As previously mentioned, one of the main benefits associated with an RRSP is that the playing field becomes level since a unified tax system applies for all securities held within the account. By holding the security with the largest tax burden within an account that levels the playing field, the investor's overall tax liability should be minimized.

- **Note**: At this point, you may be curious as to why we would not choose to hold interest-paying securities within a TFSA since the tax liability would be eliminated entirely. Of course, this option would also be ideal. However, given the extremely low TFSA contribution room available relative to that of RRSPs and non-registered accounts, most investors are likely to hold a majority of their investment securities within an RRSP or a non-registered. Therefore, the more relevant comparison from an Asset Allocation perspective is whether to allocate a specific asset class towards an RRSP or a

---

[5] Refer to end of chapter note

non-registered. With that being said, since the tax reduction benefits of the TFSA are so similar to that of the RRSP, it is safe to assume that if a security should be held within an RRSP over a non-registered, it should also be held within a TFSA over a non-registered, and vice versa. A more relevant discussion of TFSAs versus RRSPs surrounds the topic of whether an investor should prioritize making contributions to their TFSA or to their RRSP. In this case, the ultimate trade off is whether the investor would prefer liquidity provided by the TFSA over the taxable income reduction associated with making a contribution to his or her RRSP. While this discussion is important, it is beyond the scope of this book.

Non-Income Producing Securities (Return Derived Solely from Capital Gains

Securities that generate a return entirely through capital gains should ideally be held within the investor's non-registered account for the following three reasons[6]:

---

[6] Refer to end of chapter note

1) The investor has complete control over the timing of their tax liability. Therefore, it would be optimal to hold as many of the investor's interest-paying and dividend-paying securities (those where the investor has zero control over the tax liability) within an RRSP (or TFSA) and hold the securities where the investor has control (non-income paying securities) within a non-registered.

2) For investors with a higher marginal tax rate than the effective tax rate for capital gains, selling a security, realizing the gain, and then withdrawing the proceeds from the account would result in a larger tax liability if the security was held within an RRSP.

3) Equity securities that do not pay a dividend and strictly provide investors with a return on capital can arguably be regarded as riskier (we will expand on this topic in Chapter 8). Therefore, if any of these securities end up losing value, the investor can use the capital losses to offset capital gains and lower their overall tax liability. In an RRSP or TFSA, the investor cannot make use of this strategy.

Dividend-Paying Equity Securities

As for equity investments that pay a dividend, ideally, it would be beneficial to hold these securities within an RRSP since the investor would gain control over the timing of their tax liability[7]. With that being said, it is important to remember that the magnitude of the tax liability for dividend paying securities is lower than that for interest paying securities as a result of the preferential tax treatment provided to shareholders in dividend paying companies. Therefore, if the investor has a large enough portfolio to the point where the dividend-paying securities could only be held in the RRSP at the expense of holding interest-paying securities, the dividend-paying securities should be held within the non-registered since the investor's overall tax liability would be higher if the interest-paying securities were held within the non-registered.

In the following chapter, we will discuss the final two threats to our financial wealth: **the media and the investor**. Following this, we will introduce the benefits of Dividend Growth Investing and explain why it is the most

---

[7] Refer to end of chapter note

efficient investment solution to combat each of the many threats to our financial wealth.

End of Chapter Note

Please note, readers should seek independent tax guidance from a tax professional prior to implementing any of the tax strategies introduced in this chapter.

Chapter Five

The Media and the Investor

I am somewhat ashamed to admit that my first visit to a Costco store was only a couple of years ago, shortly after a new store opened in my neighborhood. Naturally, curiosity got the best of me and I just had to experience firsthand what the excitement was all about.

What I remember most from that first visit was that my enormous shopping cart, the size of a mini-dumpster used for home renovations, overflowed with bulk-sized items – large pails of Nutella, jumbo bags of my favourite late night salty snack, 72 rolls of bathroom tissue, cereal boxes the size of carry-on luggage, and even a few cases of a popular albacore tuna that piqued my interest at the time. The single common factor amongst these items was that they were priced around 30% lower than what I was accustomed to paying. **Almost instinctively, I was inclined to "stock up" on these items**.

At this point, you are most likely asking yourself how my

obsession with Costco is related to investing. Buried deep within that delicious jar of Nutella is an underlying investment principle that investors and the media find difficult to grasp. In every other aspect of our economic and financial lives, the societal norm taught from a very early age is that **high prices are bad** and **low prices are good**, plain and simple. In my Costco example, I was incentivized to purchase more items than I normally would because I could **purchase them at a discount**.

Unfortunately, for some inconceivable reason, this idea of **purchasing at a discount** does not resonate well with the investment community. When prices are increasing, investors are more than willing to invest in an attempt to 'join in on the rally'. When prices are decreasing, investors panic and sell their positions out of fear that prices will continue to decrease.

This reversed philosophy of buying when prices are high and selling when prices are low is not only flawed, it also has the potential to be incredibly destructive to our financial wealth. At this point, you are most likely asking yourself the same question that has haunted me for years: how did we get to this point? For over 200 years, this flawed view of investing has slowly transitioned to become a norm in the investment community as a result of the following:

1. An injustice committed by the Investment Media to cover topics that will maximize profit rather than properly inform investors.
2. Lack of responsibility from investors to keep themselves informed and follow a basic rule of thumb.

<u>The Media</u>

At the expense of its target audience, often it is in the media's best interest to cover topics that are likely to maximize viewer count rather than properly educate its audience. Time and time again we have seen this strategy put into practice, despite the fact that the only party who benefits in the end is the media themselves.

Recall the last time you watched your local news network. I am willing to bet that a majority of the topics covered were related to death, injury, robbery, or in some way associated with criminal activity. This tendency for news networks to repeatedly cover stories of this nature is certainly no coincidence. Instead, they understand that **people are subconsciously more inclined to read or watch negative news stories because they provide a unique level of what is deemed as "shock" value**. Through referencing the results of two major studies, we will make the following arguments:

> 1) A majority of the population is subconsciously more inclined to read or watch negative news headlines over positive or neutral news headlines.
>
> 2) The emotional gratification of a positive instance is lower in magnitude than the emotional toll of a negative instance; thus, negative instances provide more "shock value".

Together, these two arguments support the notion that the Investment Media can increase their viewer count by inflicting fear on the population. The Investment Media inflicts fear through two common methods:

> 1) The Investment Media spreads negative news about stocks or alternative investments that have seen recent share price decreases. Their goal is to make viewers fearful that if they do not sell soon, there is a possibility

that they may lose even more money. In reality, the underlying investment may actually be fundamentally sound.

2) The Investment Media will spread positive news about stocks or alternative investments that have seen rapid and abnormal share price increases over a short period of time. Their goal is to make viewers fearful that if they do not invest soon, they will miss out on an opportunity for significant returns. In reality, the underlying investment may, in fact, be overpriced.

Argument #1: A majority of the population is subconsciously more inclined to read or watch negative news headlines over positive or neutral news headlines.

In an attempt to determine whether people were subconsciously more inclined to view or read negative news headlines, researchers Marc Trussler and Stuart Soroka, from McGill University in Canada, set up an experiment.[xiii] To eliminate the potential for biased results, participants were advised that the point of the experiment was to study eye tracking. The volunteers were first asked to select a few stories about politics to read from a news website so that a camera could make preliminary, eye-tracking measurements prior to the experiment. The participants were told that this was simply a "preparation" phase and that it was important that they actually read the articles so that the right measurements could be prepared. **In reality, it did not matter what they read, but rather, it mattered which articles they chose to read.**

After the preparation phase, the volunteers were asked to watch a short video which they believed to be the main purpose of the experiment. In reality, the video was simply a filler and unrelated to the actual experiment. After the video, the volunteers were asked to answer questions on the type of political news they enjoy reading.

The results of the experiment showed that a majority of the participants chose to read stories with a negative tone, corruption, set-backs, hypocrisy and so on, rather than neutral or positive stories. However, when these results were compared to the participants' answers to the question "which type of political news do you enjoy reading?", the answers were, for the most part, the very opposite. Most participants who subconsciously chose to read negative news stories answered that they prefer to read positive news stories. The important insight to note is that even though most people agree that the media should cover news that is more positive and educational, their natural inclination is to pay attention to the negative headlines.

As previously mentioned, the media is already aware of this **"negativity bias"** prevalent amongst the majority of the population. Unfortunately, it is exploited in order to generate higher viewer counts, thus maximizing profits.

<u>Argument #2: The emotional gratification of a positive instance is lower in magnitude than the emotional toll of a negative instance, thus, negative instances provide more "shock value".</u>

It can also be argued that society's "negativity bias" is the result of people having a stronger desire to be "shocked" by negative news than uplifted by positive news. To further this point, another study shows that the magnitude of the negative effect of losing money, a negative instance, is greater than the magnitude of the positive effect of gaining money, a positive instance. Moreover, this notion is not limited to money, for example:

- People are more likely to become politically involved when their rights are being threatened than they would be to fight for greater human rights.
- Employees are more likely to remain at a position which lacks advancement because the risk of losing this job outweighs the reward of finding a better job.

This idea that losses have a more significant impact than gains is referred to as **"Loss Aversion"**. In the report "Frames, Biases, and Rational Decision-Making in the Human Brain" created by Benedetto De Martino, Dharshan Kumaran, Ben Seymour, and Raymond J. Dolan, an experiment was conducted that showed just how strongly a human behaviour will change if the feeling of loss is introduced.[xiv]

In this study, participants were given $50. Next, they were asked to choose between one of the following two options:

1) Keep $30, or
2) Gamble with a 50% chance of keeping or losing the entire $50.

The results showed that 43% of participants decided to gamble their money.

In the second part of the study, participants were told to choose between the following two options:

1) Lose $20, or
2) Gamble with a 50% chance of keeping or losing the entire $50.

The results were outstanding. When one of the choices was framed as a loss, the number of participants who decided to gamble grew to 61%.

The results of this study truly emphasize that society is more sensitive to negative instances than they are to positive instances. **When combined with our first argument, it can be deduced that society is more inclined to subconsciously read or view negative news stories as a result of the human behaviour to be more sensitive to negative instances than positive instances.**

Earlier in this chapter, I explained how the notion of purchasing a security at a lower price is more profitable for investors than purchasing the same security after it has already appreciated in value. Now that we have obtained the same knowledge as the Investment Media regarding society's inclination to subconsciously read or view negative news stories over positive news stories, let us pretend we are in their shoes. In doing so, we will learn to understand why I believe they are incentivized to provide investors with misguided information.

Imagine you are the head of a large investment news broadcasting company. Like the rest of the industry, your company's compensation is positively correlated to the number of views it receives. While the quality of the news may have some impact on compensation, the majority of compensation is based on view count. Now imagine your assistant presents you with the following two choices to be aired on tonight's broadcast:

> 1) A news story advocating that as a result of Stock A's recent share price decrease, investors are presented with a great opportunity to purchase more of the fundamentally sound company at a discount price.
> 2) A news story advocating that as a result of Stock A's recent share price decrease, investors are urged to cut

their losses short before it is too late and purchase Stock B, a company whose share price has done very well over the recent months.

With the knowledge we have developed regarding society's **negativity bias** and the theory of **loss aversion**, it is clear that the second news story would result in a higher view count since it inflicts fear in the eyes of the viewer. First, the viewer is led to believe that if they do not sell Stock A, they will eventually lose more money. Second, the viewer is led to believe that by not investing in Stock B, they are missing out on potential returns. Despite the fact that the second news story suggests horrible advice to viewers, we would be incentivized to air this story since it exploits society's natural tendency to view negative news over positive news, leading to higher profits for our news broadcasting company.

As for the first news story, even though the advice provided to viewers is in their best interest, it involves executing the exact opposite of what we would want to do if our goal is to maximize viewer count. Airing this story would mean taking a potential negative news headline, "Stock A's value sees sharp decline", and converting it to a positive. With society being more inclined to view negative news headlines, this action would result in less viewers and, as a result, less profit for our organization.

Unfortunately, until the compensation for these media creators transitions from "number of views" to "quality of content", we should not expect any drastic improvements any time soon.

<u>The Investor</u>

As previously mentioned, investors around the world have only added to the problem due to:

1. **Lack of education on investing**, and
2. **Abandoning the simple "rule of thumb"**.

Now that it is quite obvious that the media is not on our side, it is our responsibility to properly educate ourselves.

Only forty years ago, misinformation was a serious threat to our financial wealth because the outlets through which an individual could obtain information were extremely limited. For example, in 1978, if an individual was interested in learning about the topic of investing, he or she could do so by either watching television, listening to the radio, or reading a textbook. Unfortunately, the most fact-based, unbiased method of receiving information - reading a textbook - also happens to require the most effort. Since, on average, most people generally do not want to take the time to read a textbook, a majority of the population simply receive their information from the television or the radio. In the first subsection of this book, we illustrated just how flawed the media's motives are. Therefore, with most of the population receiving their information through television or the radio, misinformation was an extreme threat to the financial wealth of many investors.

Today, misinformation remains one of the most detrimental threats to our financial wealth. Even though technology has given us the ability to obtain information within seconds, it has also created a new issue - an abundance of discreditable information. While our main concern in the past was a limited number of information sources, the issue today has become how to distinguish between reliable and unreliable sources. As a result, investors today have a responsibility to conduct proper research and validate the reliability of their sources in order to properly educate themselves.

In addition to lack of education, investors have done a poor job at following the simple rule of thumb: **all else equal, high prices are bad and low prices are good**. When stocks decrease in price as a result of factors unrelated to the underlying company's fundamentals, investors should view this as an opportunity to increase their position in good, strong companies at a discounted price. The temporary decrease in the value of our portfolio is simply the price we pay for premium returns in the long run.

If you were to remember one piece of information from this chapter it should be this: **we, the investors, are the only ones who can destroy this flawed investment notion of buying when prices increase and selling when prices decrease since the Media is not acting in our best interests**. As we will discuss in Chapter Eight and Chapter Nine, Dividend Growth Investing is the best strategy for combatting against the threats brought upon by the media and ourselves because of its systematic approach and principal preservation qualities, which both aim to eliminate all emotion from the investment decision.

Section Three:

The Solutions

Chapter Six
Enhanced Investment Returns

"There are 60,000 economists in the U.S., many of them employed full-time trying to forecast recessions and interest rates, and if they could do it successfully twice in a row, they'd all be millionaires by now...as far as I know, most of them are still gainfully employed, which ought to tell us something." –Peter Lynch

In previous chapters, we not only introduced the threats to our financial wealth, we also went into great detail addressing the negative consequences these threats can have on our ability to save enough money to last for the entirety of our retirement years. As a reminder, here are the culprits:

- Understated Inflation
- Low Interest Rates
- Longevity Risk
- Taxes
- The Media
- The Investor

Not only are most investors unable to effectively address these threats, most are not even aware of the extent to which these threats can be detrimental. For this reason, I have dedicated the entire first half of this series to discussing these threats. I hope by this point, my readers are aware of how significant an impact these threats have on limiting our ability to grow and preserve our financial wealth.

Now that the problems have been introduced, we must now discuss a solution that will protect us against these threats. With over 25 years of experience in the investment industry, **I strongly believe that the most efficient investing methodology to protect and grow our hard earned financial wealth is Dividend Growth Investing**.

Over the course of Section Three, we will discuss the benefits of Dividend Growth Investing and how this style of investing addresses each and every threat to our financial wealth.

The Road to Victory: Choose the Winners First and the Losers Last

Like most kids, the most anticipated, sought out part of my elementary school days was the none other than **recess**. Racing out to the playground, taking on new adventures with friends; that one-hour break after lunch felt almost magical.

Every so often, my friends and I would spend our recess playing soccer. We would race out to the field and almost immediately, two captains would be selected. The two captains would then take turns choosing from a group of players to join their teams. Naturally, the captains would choose players on a scale of descending skill level. In other words, the best players would be chosen first and the worse players would be chosen last.

At this point, you are probably curious as to where I am headed with this story about my childhood days. Nostalgic? Yes. However, I promise there is a connection to investment management with this story.

How did each captain assess the skill level of each player prior to choosing them to join their team? Clearly, each player did not have numbers drawn on their foreheads representing the number of goals, assists, and overall contribution they would bring to the game ahead. Instead, **their skill level was assessed based on the captains' interpretation of the players' average performance over previous games.**

Similar to this classic case of kids constructing soccer teams for recess; one of the most important variables to consider when choosing which investment strategy to employ is the strategy's past performance. If a strategy has, on average, performed well over a period of more than twenty years, we can rest assured knowing that the strategy is likely to exhibit similar performance over future periods.

As we will discuss over the duration of this chapter, one of the solutions to combat against the many threats to our financial wealth is the fact that, on average, Dividend Growth Investing has produced **significantly higher investment returns** than that of interest paying securities, multiple versions of equities, mutual funds, and real estate investing. **In other words, Dividend Growth Investing is the first player to join the soccer team at recess.**

Dividend Growth Investing vs. Interest-Paying Securities

In Chapter Two, we introduced the first two threats to our financial wealth, understated inflation and low interest rates. As discussed, the government may be incentivized to understate inflation because government pension payments are linked to inflation. To make matters worse, since interest rates are correlated to inflation and, as a result, have been extremely low, interest paying securities such as GICs do not provide a return that exceeds the real rate of inflation. **The combined effects of understated inflation and low interest rates is detrimental to investors because our interest-paying investments will simply not be able to generate a return sufficient enough to keep up with the real rate of inflation; therefore, our wealth will deteriorate over time.**

To provide concrete evidence to support this notion, let us compare the ten-year annual average return generated by the WisdomTree Canada Quality Dividend Growth Index, a fundamentally weighted index that measures the performance of 50 dividend-paying Canadian companies with growth characteristics, to that of the S&P Canada Aggregate Bond Index:

- WisdomTree Canada Quality Dividend Growth Index: 10.94%[8]
- S&P Canada Aggregate Bond Index: 3.82%[9]

As expected, the WisdomTree Canada Quality Dividend Growth Index generated an annual average return significantly higher than that generated by the average fixed income security over the past ten years. This comparison should be regarded as no more than a formality considering the fact that we have already provided an extensive amount of evidence in earlier chapters which illustrated the inferior returns provided by fixed income securities.

Dividend Growth Investing vs. All Other Equity Classes

As it is now quite evident that Dividend Growth Investing has historically outperformed the average fixed income

---

[8] From December 31st 2008 to December 31st, 2018
[9] From December 31st 2008 to December 31st, 2018

security, let us analyze how Dividend Growth Investing has stacked up against all other equity classes. The following graph compares the growth of $1,000,000 from 1986 to 2016 for different companies within the world of equities:

Growth of $1,000,000 from 1986 to 2016

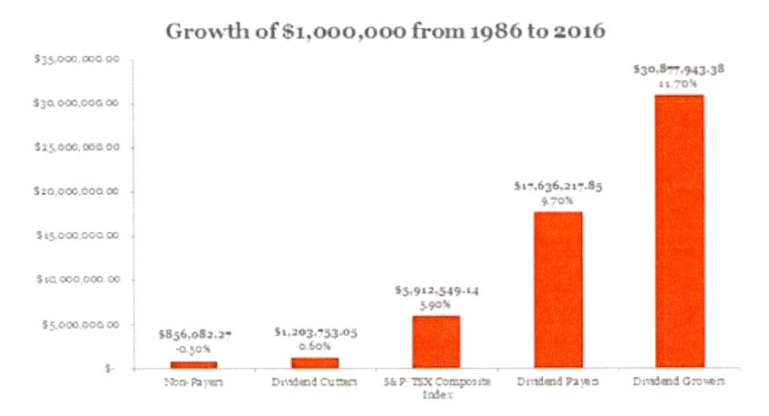

Category	Value	%
Non-Payers	$856,082.27	-0.50%
Dividend Cutters	$1,203,753.05	0.60%
S&P TSX Composite Index	$5,912,549.14	5.90%
Dividend Payers	$17,636,217.85	9.70%
Dividend Growers	$30,877,943.38	11.70%

Figure A6: Growth of $1,000,000 from 1986 to 2016 for different companies within the world of equities.[xv]

As you can see from *Figure A6*, Dividend Growth companies have historically provided a return significantly higher than that provided by all other forms of equity. In addition, the return generated by Dividend Growth companies has historically exceeded both the rate of inflation suggested by the government and the, much higher, real inflation rate estimated in Chapter Two. In others words, **investing in companies that have the ability to grow their dividends allows investors to**

increase the value of their wealth rather than have their purchasing power deteriorate over time.

Whether you consider yourself to be an expert or beginner in the world of investments, I think we can all agree that one of the most important factors to consider when deciding on whether or not to pursue a certain investment opportunity is past performance. After viewing *Figure A6*, why would any rational individual invest in non-dividend paying companies for long-term growth when the returns have historically been significantly inferior to that of companies that have grown their dividends? The reality is that most people disregard past performance when determining which companies to invest in and fail to execute proper due diligence. This single shortcoming demonstrated by most investors is the main reason mutual funds are still present after all these years, despite notoriously underperforming their benchmark time and time again.

Dividend Growth Investing vs. Mutual Funds

Before we conduct this comparison, it is important to understand the nature of how a mutual fund operates.

Mutual funds, also referred to as "open-ended funds" provide investors with the ability to diversify their wealth across a number of unique equities and fixed income securities by purchasing units or shares of an investment pool. This investment pool is then managed and controlled by a fund manager on behalf of the investors.

For example, we will assume Investor A, Investor B, Investor C, and Investor D each have $250,000 to invest but are unsure as to how to go about investing their wealth. For the sake of simplicity, we will assume fees, taxes, and fund expenses do not exist. One day, a fund manager approaches the investors, offers to invest each investor's $250,000 on their behalf, and pools the money together in preparation of investing the cash into various investment securities. In other words, the fund manager has just created a mutual fund. At this point, the fund is valued at $1,000,000 since the total assets under management are worth $1,000,000 ($250,000 provided by each of the four investors). The fund manager then splits the $1,000,000 into 100,000 units. As a result, each unit is worth $10 and each investor receives 25,000 units, coinciding with the total $250,000 they each originally invested.

Now that the fund is established, the fund manager is able to invest the $1,000,000 across various investment securities. At the end of each day, the value of the fund's price per unit is recalculated, with the value dependent on the value of the underlying investments. For example, we will assume that at the end of the first day, the fund realizes a gain of 1.50%. As a result, the fund's price per unit is recalculated as follows:

- The fund's assets grew from $1,000,000 to $1,015,000.
- The value of the fund's assets, $1,015,000, is divided by the number of units outstanding, 100,000.
- **New Unit Price = $10.15**

For each of the original four investors, the new value of their total investment (25,000 units x $10.15) is calculated to be $253,750.

Now assume that after the first day, a fifth investor enters the scene, Investor E. She wishes to invest a total of $100,000 into the fund. Since each unit is now valued at $10.15, her $100,000 investment provides her with 9852 fund units. The net effect of the additional investor on the overall fund is illustrated in the following text:

- The fund's assets would grow from $1,015,000 to $1,115,000.
- The fund's number of units outstanding would grow from 100,000 units to 109,852 units.
- The fund's price per unit would remain the same at $10.15.

The purpose of introducing a new investor in our example was to show that despite the fact that individual investors have the ability to contribute or redeem their units, the change in the fund's total value will always be proportional to the number of units added or subtracted; therefore, the price per unit remains unaffected.

Now that we have reviewed the nature of how mutual funds operate, let us proceed to analyze their historical performance.

At the beginning of 2018, the Globe and Mail, Canada's most widely used news source, published an article comparing the 10-year annual average return for Canada's

50 largest mutual funds. The following graph compares the 10-year annual average return of the ten largest mutual funds in Canada to the 10-year annual average return generated by the Royal Bank of Canada, a Dividend Growth stock:

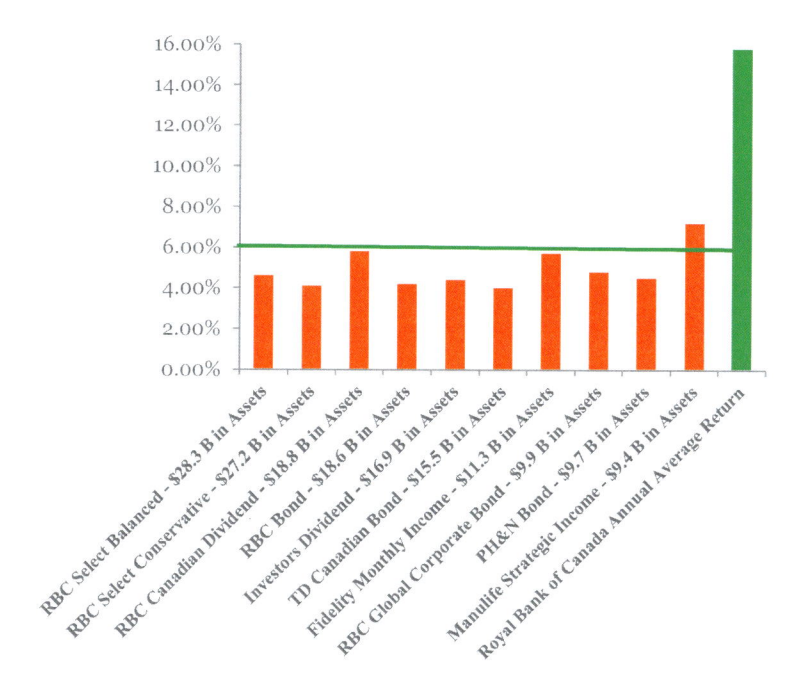

Figure B6: 10-year annual average return of ten largest Canadian mutual funds compared to 10-year annual average return of the Royal Bank of Canada's stock[10,xvi]

Before we compare the results, it is important to explain the significance of the green horizontal line drawn along the

---

[10] From December 31st, 2007 to December 31st, 2017

six percent mark. This line represents our real inflation rate, a figure we estimated back in Chapter Two. Almost unbelievably, the 10-year annual average return generated by nine out of ten of Canada's largest mutual funds came out to be below six percent. To further emphasize this point, **$156.20 billion worth of savings failed to grow at a pace greater than the real rate of inflation, consequently resulting in a significant loss of purchasing power for millions of Canadians**.

Let us now take a look at Royal Bank of Canada's stock performance over the same 10-year period. From 2007 to 2017, the Royal Bank of Canada's stock generated an annual average return of roughly 16%, far surpassing the rate of return generated by Canada's top ten mutual funds. It should be clear that *Figure B6* is a simple graph that illustrates a very powerful point: **Canadians who had simply purchased shares in the Royal Bank of Canada would have generated a significantly higher return than the return generated by the mutual funds offered by the bank itself.** It does not surprise me that the Royal Bank of Canada, the company who generated a 10-year annual average return of more than double that of the top ten

Canadian mutual funds, just so happens to be a Dividend Growth company.

Even when we compare the ten-year annual average return generated by the average Top 10 Canadian mutual funds to the 10.94% return generated by the WisdomTree Canada Quality Dividend Growth Index, an index we introduced earlier in this chapter, it becomes evident that the Royal Bank of Canada is not the only one who has outperformed mutual funds. Rather, Canadian Dividend Growth stocks as a whole have, on average, outperformed mutual funds over the last 10 years.

This evidence raises the very predictable follow up question: what factors have led mutual funds to underperform when compared to individual stocks? While the master list is certainly long, we will limit our discussion to the following three contributors:

1) Over-Diversification
2) Cash Drag
3) Loss of control over timing of capital gains tax liability

As illustrated through our example provided earlier, new investors are able to purchase new units in mutual funds at any point in time. In doing so, new assets are added to the fund which will be invested into various investment securities by the fund manager. Certain regulations apply that restrict the number of shares or units fund managers are able to purchase, primarily to prevent fund companies from obtaining a majority share in the underlying firm. If you recall from *Figure B6*, seven of Canada's largest mutual funds have assets under management in excess of $10 billion. If a $10 billion fund were to allocate just five percent of their assets towards a publically traded company valued at $1 billion, the fund would essentially obtain a 50% ownership in the firm. Since an ownership stake of this magnitude would result in a conflict of interest, fund managers are forced to abide by the strict rules and mandates governed by the securities regulators. Unfortunately for investors, the end result is an overly diversified investment fund made up of unfavourable securities.

Mason Hawkins, a well-known value investor, strongly advocates that in order for a portfolio to achieve sufficient diversification, it should be made up of roughly 18 to 22 securities.[xvii] Unfortunately for a majority of mutual funds, this range is simply impossible to achieve without obtaining a majority ownership in the underlying companies. As a result, these funds are forced to diversify their holdings amongst, in some cases, hundreds of different securities.

In addition to the restrictions placed on the security selection process, fund managers are also required to maintain a certain proportion of assets in the form of cash. The purpose of this requirement is to satisfy investor redemptions and to maintain liquidity for future purchases. However, fees charged to investors are charged as a percentage of the fund's total assets, despite the fact that the cash portion of the fund provides the investor with no potential return. According to a study conducted by William O'Reilly, CFA and Michael Preisano, CFA, this wrongful overcharge, also referred to as **Cash Drag**, costs investors 0.83% of their portfolio value on an annual basis.[xviii]

When investors purchase a unit in a mutual fund, not only do they give up control of their investment portfolio, they also give up control over the timing of their capital gains tax liability. As explained in Chapter 4, the investor usually has complete control over the timing of their capital gains tax since taxes are only charged once the investor decides to sell their security. Mutual fund unit holders, however, relinquish that control over purchases and sales made within the fund. Unfortunately, they are still liable for the associated capital gains taxes which are automatically passed through to the unit holder on a periodic basis. In other words, the unit holder's lack of control over purchases and sales leads to a lack of control over the timing of their tax liability.

At this point, it is quite evident that the enhanced investment returns historically provided by Dividend Growth companies have far exceeded the historical returns provided by interest paying securities, all other equity classes, and mutual funds. It is surprising, then, that, **despite the fact that Dividend Growth investing is a long-term, slow, and conservative approach to investing, society continues to view this methodology as highly speculative by nature because of its association with the stock market.** For some inconceivable reason, society has grouped all stock market related investments under the umbrella of highly speculative, gambling-equivalents, even though the characteristics of two separate stocks trading on the stock market can vary drastically. As an example, let us consider the following two companies:

- **Company A**: A penny stock with zero revenue, negative earnings, under financial distress, and a market value of $0.100 billion based solely on promises management has made to shareholders.
- **Company B**: The Royal Bank of Canada, one of the largest banks in the world with a market value of $155 billion.

Think about how ridiculous it would be to view Company A under the same umbrella as Company B. Stock A's underlying company has no proven track record, no operations, and a value based entirely on investor sentiment. In the event that only a handful of major investors lose faith in the company, the stock price is likely to crash down, as the share price cannot gravitate to a fundamental share value.

On the other hand, Stock B's underlying company is a strong, established, Dividend Growth company, with a proven track record of positive performance for over 100 years. The company operates globally, generates strong, sustainable earnings year after year, and has a strong foundation which enables it to continuously expand its operations. In addition, the dividend provided acts as a cushion to the company's share price in the event of a market correction. We will expand on this topic in Chapter Eight.

Clearly, the societal view of placing all stock market activity under the umbrella of "highly speculative" is extremely flawed. In fact, as opposed to being compared to the other classes of equities shown in *Figure A6*, I strongly believe a more suitable comparison would be to Real Estate Investing - a long-term, slow, yet rewarding approach to investing.

Dividend Growth Investing vs. Real Estate Investing

Real Estate Investing has been highly regarded as one of the most powerful methods to grow wealth over the long run, and rightfully so. For example, as most Canadians are aware, Toronto real estate has skyrocketed in value over the past few decades. For the sake of making a comparison, let us compare the total return provided by a $50,000 investment in an average Toronto home back in 1973 to a

$50,000 investment in shares of TD Bank, a Dividend Growth company, during the same time period:

Average Price of a 3-Bedroom Toronto Home vs. TD Shares from 1973-2018

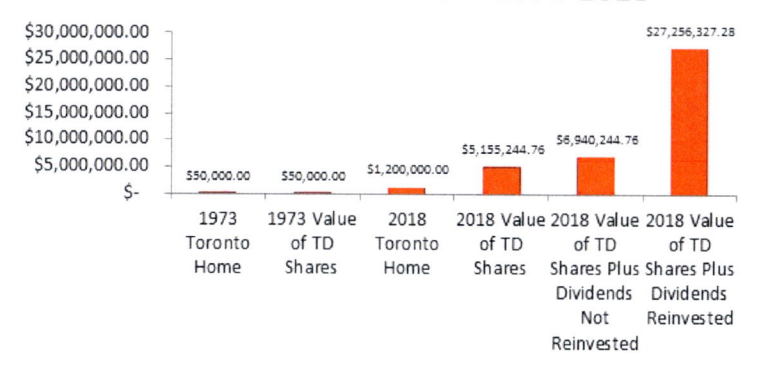

1973 Toronto Home	$50,000.00
1973 Value of TD Shares	$50,000.00
2018 Toronto Home	$1,200,000.00
2018 Value of TD Shares	$5,155,244.76
2018 Value of TD Shares Plus Dividends Not Reinvested	$6,940,244.76
2018 Value of TD Shares Plus Dividends Reinvested	$27,256,327.28

Figure C6: Average Price of 3-Bedroom Toronto Home versus TD bank shares from 1973 to 2018.[xix]

As shown from *Figure C6*, a Toronto home valued at $50,000 in 1973 has grown to, on average, $1,200,000 in 2018, not a bad return when viewed on its own. However, when we compare that return to the return of TD Bank shares over the same time period, with dividends reinvested, the power of Dividend Growth Investing clearly becomes evident. From 1973 to 2018, $50,000 worth of TD Bank shares would have grown to an incredible $27,256,327.28 with dividends reinvested. Without reinvesting the dividends and simply leaving them in cash, the combined value of TD Bank shares and the cash dividends would amount to $6,940,244.76, still, nearly five times the value of a Toronto home.

Most people would be overwhelmingly surprised to find out that the return of a bank stock could outperform Toronto real estate by such a large margin over a 45-year period, let alone outperform Toronto real estate at all. Once again, the reason why most individuals would view this fact as surprising is a result of society's classification of all stocks as short-term, highly speculative investments. In other words, society has engraved the notion that the saying "you may win at a casino once, maybe twice, but in the long term, the house always wins" applies to the stock market. Put simply, I would argue that this is singularly the most inaccurate representation of what true investing in the stock market is all about. **The most efficient way to invest in the stock market is to identify fundamentally sound companies that have demonstrated the ability to grow their earnings and dividends over a long period of time**.

While the primary focus of this chapter is on the investment returns of Dividend Growth Investing, I believe now would be an appropriate time to make an honorable mention of a few additional advantages of Dividend Growth Investing over Real Estate Investing:

- More liquidity
- No tenants
- No maintenance issues
- Less complicated estate planning
- Easier diversification strategies

We have now compared the enhanced investment returns of Dividend Growth Investing to:

1) Interest Paying Securities
2) All Other Equity Classes
3) Mutual Funds
4) Real Estate Investing

In all four cases, Dividend Growth companies have historically provided investors with the highest level of investment returns.

Chapter Seven

The Power of Yield on Cost

"I'm a conservative investor; I don't want to risk losing my entire retirement savings…"

…It seems as though it was just yesterday that I heard these words for the very first time.

In 2009, a close friend of mine asked for my opinion on whether or not he should purchase a GIC to replace his stock portfolio. Despite the extremely low historical returns provided by GICs relative to the historical returns generated by other investments, he was obsessed with the idea of obtaining a "guaranteed return" with zero volatility. Considering the fact that the entire world was in a state of recovery from the financial crisis of 2008, I understood his concern. **He, along with many other investors, had simply lost confidence in the financial markets**.

As I have reiterated countless times throughout this book, **market corrections provide investors with an**

opportunity to purchase fundamentally sound companies at a discounted price. But imagine how difficult it was to motivate others to conform to this philosophy during one of the largest market corrections of all time. No matter how many attempts I made to explain this idea to my friend, he simply could not wrap his head around the concept.

Leveraging the fact that my friend had many years of experience with Real Estate Investing, I decided to take an alternative approach. The very next time we met for coffee, I simply asked whether or not he would purchase an investment property based on the following conditions:

- A $5,000,000 apartment building which must be held for the next 25 years.
- For the entire investment period, rental income would be capped at 2% of the initial property value ($100,000/year).
- At the end of 25 years, the investor would be able to sell the property for no more than $5,000,000.
- The investor is guaranteed 100% tenant occupancy for the entire investment period. In other words, an annual income stream of $100,000 is guaranteed for 25 years.

After giving my proposal a quick review, he looked at me with a confused expression on his face. I will never forget his response:

"Who in their right mind would purchase this building? The fact that the rent would be capped in the first year of the investment is dreadful, not to mention that the property value would remain stagnant over a period of 25 years!"

Moments later, my friend quickly realized what I had accomplished. I had tricked him into answering his own question regarding whether or not he should replace his stock portfolio with a GIC. With this simple example, he finally understood the notion that **his desire to have "guaranteed returns" would come at an even larger cost: inferior long term returns**. At the same time, it became clear that the **short term market fluctuations he experienced when investing in stocks and real estate were simply the costs necessary to achieve superior returns in the long run**.

At this point, you may have picked up on the fact that traditional GICs have identical investment properties to that of the hypothetical real estate investment previously introduced. To recap, the main components of a traditional GIC are as follows:

- The annual interest payments are paid as a fixed percentage of the investor's original principal for the entire investment period. In other words, interest payments remain static for the entire investment period.
- At maturity, the investor's principal is returned without any capital appreciation.

In Chapter Three, we focused our attention on one of the many negatives associated with GICs - the inability to make use of the Power of Compound Interest. Since the annual percentage return generated by a GIC is based solely off the original principal rather than off the original principal plus previously generated returns, GICs pose a huge threat to an investor's ability to generate superior returns over a long period of time.

In this chapter, we will focus our attention on an additional issue with GICs and other securities that pay a non-growing income stream - **the inability to create an indexed pension that grows at a faster rate than inflation**. To fairly compare GICs and other non-growing income paying securities to Dividend Growth stocks, we will remove the effects of compound interest by making the following two assumptions for all examples used within this chapter:

1) No securities, including stocks, generate capital appreciation.
- **Note**: If you recall from previous chapters, an investor's total return is broken down into two components:
    i) Return from capital appreciation
    ii) Return from income
- This chapter will focus solely on the income portion of total return, or in other words, the portion of the return paid to investors in the form of cash.

2) All investment income (interest and dividends) generated by a security is withdrawn from the account and used by the investor to cover everyday expenditures. In other words, the investment income generated from the security will be the investor's sole source of income.

With these two assumptions in effect, securities that take advantage of the Power of Compounding Interest will not be able to do so since there will be no previously generated returns from which to compound. Instead, for all securities, the percentage return will be based solely off the original principal. These simple assumptions provide an equal playing field between *simple interest* securities such as the traditional GIC and *compound interest* securities such as Dividend Growth stocks. With an equal playing field, we will be able to fairly prove why securities generating a fixed income stream (Ex: GICs, traditional bonds, non-growth dividend stocks) are inferior to securities capable of generating a growing income stream (Ex: Dividend Growth stocks) with regards to providing investors with an indexed pension surpassing the rate of inflation.

To carry out this comparison, the remainder of this chapter will follow this structure:

> 1) First, we will introduce the concept of Yield on Cost and explain how it can be used to compare the growth of investment income across different investments.
> 2) Second, we will compare the Yield on Cost for a portfolio that pays a fixed income stream, a portfolio made up of GICs, to that of a portfolio that pays a growing income stream, a Dividend Growth portfolio.

This example will illustrate the extent to which how much more effective securities capable of generating a growing income stream are at creating an indexed pension than securities that pay a fixed income stream. 3) Third, we will show the Yield on Cost for multiple Dividend Growth companies to provide real world evidence of this concept.

What is Yield on Cost?

The yield on cost ratio allows investors to compare the growth in investment income over time between multiple investments. The ratio is calculated as follows:

$$Yield\ on\ Cost = \frac{Annualized\ Dividend\ or\ Interest\ in\ Most\ Recent\ Year}{Original\ Principal}$$

For example, let us assume an investor purchases a security for $1,000 to be held for a five-year period. The annual income provided by the investment over the entire investment period is illustrated as follows:

Year 1: $50
Year 2: $75
Year 3: $100

Year 4: $125

Year 5: $150

In Year 0, the point at which the investor contemplates whether or not he would like to pursue the investment, he is aware that if he were to invest $1,000, his annual return in Year 1 would amount to $50. As a result, his investment yield would be 5%.

We will assume that the investor had decided to pursue the investment and has now been invested for four out of five years. At this point, he decides he would like to evaluate how much his investment income has grown thus far over the investment period. He decides to analyze this growth by calculating his Yield on Cost. He divides his $125 annual income by the original $1,000 principal, consistent with the Yield on Cost formula, and arrives at 12.5%. At this point in time, with an original investment of only $1,000, the investor's investment is able to provide him with an annual income of $125, or in percentage terms, 12.5% of his original investment. When we compare this yield on cost to the original 5% yield in Year One, it becomes evident that the investor's annual income has grown by a total of 150%.

At this point, you may be curious as to why the investor did not simply subtract his annual dollar return generated in the fourth year by the annual dollar return generated in the first year. While this method may be adequate for evaluating the growth in investment income for one security on its own, it provides little insight when comparing the growth in investment income across multiple securities because it does not account for the size of the original investment. For example, let us assume we have two securities, Investment A and Investment B. Investment A requires an original investment of $10,000 and Investment B requires an original investment of $1,000. Over a five-year period, Investment A's annual income increases from $500 per year to $1,000 per year. On the other hand, Investment B's annual income increases from $50 per year to $200 per year. If we were to simply compare the increase in investment income in dollar terms for both investments, it seems as though Investment A increased its annual income payment by more than Investment B. Of course, this conclusion would be incorrect since this comparison does not account for the fact that the original investment required for Investment A was substantially higher than that required for Investment B. Yield on Cost conducts the comparison on a per original dollar invested basis, eliminating the effect of differing original investment amounts. In this example, Investment B's yield on cost is, in fact, 20% versus Investment A's yield on cost of 10%. We can now subtract each investment's yield in Year One by the coinciding yield on costs calculated in Year Four to determine which investment truly realized a larger increase in investment income over the five-year period. Since Investment B's yield on cost in Year Four was 300% higher than its yield in Year 1 but Investment A's yield on cost in Year Four was only 100% higher than its yield in Year One, we can conclude that the increases in investment income for Investment B over the five-year period were larger than Investment A.

Now that we understand why Yield on Cost is the most effective method for comparing the growth in investment income for two separate investments, we will now compare the Yield on Cost for a portfolio that pays a fixed income stream, a portfolio made up of GICs, to that of a portfolio that pays a growing income stream, a Dividend Growth portfolio.

Yield on Cost Comparison: GIC Portfolio vs. Dividend Growth Portfolio

As we know, many investors in their retirement years consider their investment income to be their main source of income. If our investment income cannot keep up with the rate of inflation, it becomes impossible to continue to fund the same lifestyle we were once able to afford in previous years since our purchasing power diminishes year after year. For this reason, securities that generate a fixed income stream, such as GICs, are extremely susceptible to the effects of inflation since prices of goods and services grow at the inflation rate but the investor's annual income grows at zero percent. At this point, the only way for the investor to continue to support his or her existing lifestyle is to sell a portion of his or her investments and, consequently, **increase the risk of outliving his or her retirement savings.**

A dividend that has the ability to grow at a faster rate than the rate of inflation is the solution that allows investors to enjoy their existing lifestyle without the need to ever sell their original principal. **Since the dividend grows at a faster rate than the rate at which inflation erodes our** purchasing power, a **Dividend Growth strategy provides a growing income stream year after year, even after we account for the effects of inflation**. In other words, I believe **Dividend Growth Investing completely eliminates the risk of outliving our retirement savings by allowing our money to work for us.**

To expand on these points, let us compare the yield on cost of a $1,000,000 GIC portfolio to that of a $1,000,000 Dividend Growth Portfolio. Remember, staying consistent with our assumptions listed earlier in this chapter, the following assumptions will apply:

1) The share prices of the Dividend Growth stocks within the Dividend Growth portfolio do not appreciate in value.

2) The investor uses 100% of his investment income for everyday expenditures.

The first assumption does not apply in the case for our GIC portfolio since, as we have mentioned countless times throughout this book, GICs do not provide investors with capital appreciation.

GIC Portfolio

- **Yield Today: 2%**
- Average Annual Growth Rate: 0%
- **Yield on Cost in 25 years: 2%**

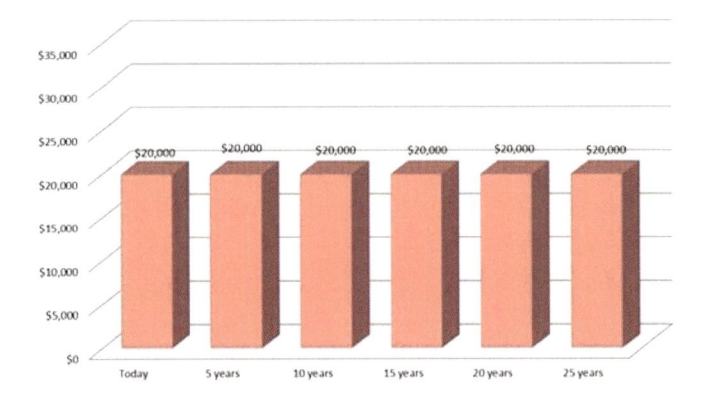

Figure A7: Interest generated from a $1,000,000 investment in a GIC portfolio over a 25-year period.

Dividend Growth Portfolio

- $1,000,000 invested in a Dividend Growth Portfolio today
- **Yield Today: 3.5%**
- Annual Average Dividend Growth Rate: 8%
- **Yield on Cost in 25 years: 23.97%**

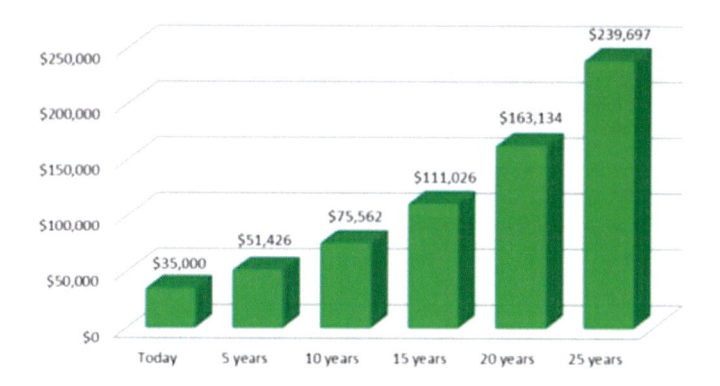

Figure A7: Dividends generated from a $1,000,000 investment in a Dividend Growth portfolio over a 25-year period.

As illustrated in *Figure A7*, the GIC portfolio pays out a fixed interest rate throughout the entire investment period; therefore, its yield on cost remains static for all 25 years and, consequently, the interest paid does not keep up with the rate of inflation. In the case of the Dividend Growth portfolio, the dividends grow at an annual average rate of 8% which leads to a yield on cost of 23.97% in the 25th year. At the end of 25 years, the dividends alone have provided the investor with two incredible benefits:

1) The dividends grew at a rate faster than the rate of inflation; therefore, the investor did not need to tap into his/her original principal in order to fund his/her lifestyle.

2) The investor now holds a conservative portfolio that generates an annual income yield of 23.97%, a risk/reward trade-off that simply cannot be attained in the marketplace. Instead, this premium risk/reward trade-off is the investors compensation for remaining invested for such a long period of time.

This example illustrates the results in a way that makes it almost inconceivable to think that anyone would make a long-term investment in a security that pays a fixed income stream. The difference in yield on costs is so significant that any benefit associated with holding the security that pays a fixed income stream over the security that is capable of increasing the income stream on an annual basis is simply not justified.

It is one thing to make the assumption that a $1,000,000 Dividend Growth portfolio will be able to grow its dividends by 8% over a 25-year period. To test the legitimacy of this claim, the next section will evaluate the Year 10 yield on cost for three real-life Canadian Dividend Growth companies over the period from 2006 to 2016. In addition to the returns generated from the dividends, the returns generated from share price appreciation have also been included to emphasize the overall power of Dividend

Growth Investing.

The Royal Bank of Canada

- **$1,000,000 invested in Royal Bank in January 2006 at a share price of $44.53**
- Yield in 2006: 3.23%
    - Yield in 2006 ($): $32,300
- 10-Year Average Annual Dividend Growth Rate: 8.45%
- Yield on Cost 2016: 7.28%
    - Yield on Cost 2016 ($): $72,800
- Share Price Appreciation 2006-2016: 126%
- **Summary**: The annual dividend of $32,300 in 2006 grew to $72,800 by 2016. In addition, the share price appreciated by 126% during this same period.

Canadian National Railway

- **$1,000,000 invested in Canadian National Railway in January 2006 at a share price of $25.75**
- Yield in 2006: 1.28%
    - Yield in 2006 ($): $12,800
- 10-Year Average Annual Dividend Growth Rate: 16.35%
- Yield on Cost 2016: 5.83%
    - Yield on Cost 2016 ($): $58,300
- Share Price Appreciation 2006-2016: 297%
- **Summary**: The annual dividend of $12,800 in 2006 grew to $58,300 by 2016. In addition, the share price appreciated by 297% during this same period.

CCL Industries

- **$1,000,000 invested in CCL Industries in January 2006 at a share price of $6.02**
- Yield in 2006: 7.14%
    - Yield in 2006 ($): $71,400
- 10-Year Average Annual Dividend Growth Rate: 16.62%
- Yield on Cost 2016: 33.22%
    - Yield on Cost 2016 ($): $332,200
- Share Price Appreciation 2006-2016: 964%
- **Summary**: The annual dividend of $71,400 in 2006 grew to $332,200 by 2016. In addition, the share price appreciated by 964% during this same period.

As previously mentioned, Dividend Growth Investing allows investors to eliminate the risk of outliving their retirement savings, contingent on the company's ability to grow their dividends at a rate faster than the rate of inflation. As illustrated, Royal Bank of Canada, Canadian National Railway, and CCL Industries demonstrated the ability to do exactly this over the past ten years.

Unfortunately, most investors tend to disregard dividends and instead concentrate entirely on stock prices. In the short run, it is recommended that the bouncing principal of a Dividend Growth portfolio should be disregarded, as it is, for the most part, a reflection of market noise. In the long run, a company's ability to grow their dividends over time will dictate which direction their stock price is headed since a company's ability to pay dividends is contingent on their ability to generate earnings. **In other words, the combined effects of healthy earnings growth and dividend growth drive a company's stock price in the long run**.

In Chapter Six, we explained how Dividend Growth companies have historically generated superior total returns than that generated by fixed income securities, all other equity classes, mutual funds, and Real Estate Investing. In chapters that came before, we explained how Dividend Growth Investing takes advantage of the Power of Compound Interest, a very significant contributing factor to Dividend Growth Investing's superior long-term returns. In this chapter, we focused entirely on explaining just how significant the investment income growth component truly is and its overall contribution to the Dividend Growth approach. In Chapter Eight, we will introduce arguably the most important factor that contributes to Dividend Growth Investing's ability to generate superior returns over a long-term investment period.

Chapter Eight

Principal Preservation

"Rule No.1: Never lose money. Rule No.2: Never forget rule No.1." **- Warren Buffett**

In Chapter Six, I introduced the process by which my friends and I would go about constructing soccer teams back in elementary school. While the concept of choosing the best players first and the worst player's last makes sense, our skill assessment of each player was, unfortunately, flawed. Rather than construct a team consisting of both defensive and offensive players, we would simply choose the players who were most likely to score first. **The issue with this strategy is that we would end up with a team of all offensive players and no defensive players.**

In its simplest form, effective portfolio management employs very similar strategies to those used by the most successful sports teams. In hockey, the main objective is to score goals against an opposing team while preventing goals against our own net. In baseball, we want to attain as many runs as possible while limiting the number of runs scored by the opposing team. Even in tennis, we want to hit the ball past the opposing player while protecting our own side.

The common trend amongst these sports is simple: **in order to be victorious, one must master both offensive and defensive facets of the game**. Especially when competing against the best, it will never be sufficient to have mastered just one of the two. Put simply, defensive strategies are just as important as offensive strategies. I am sure we can all remember a dynasty hockey team that should have won it all if it were not for their poor goaltending.

In portfolio management, **the market index is the opposing team**. In order to win, our portfolio must generate a higher annualized return than the market index over a long investment period. After 25 years of experience, I have learned that this superior return can only be generated by employing a combination of both offensive and defensive strategies. During periods where the market is in an upwards trend, the goal is to ensure our portfolio has the ability to generate returns at a rate greater than the market index. All actions that work towards achieving this goal are placed under the umbrella of **offensive strategies**.

However, above average returns during *bull markets* (periods where the market is in an upwards trend) can be completely offset by larger than average losses during market corrections. Unfortunately, for far too long, the investment community has done a poor job of recognizing the importance of principal preservation and has, instead, focused on stocks that possess significant offensive potential. For example, as of the time of writing this book, the latest buzz in the investment community surrounds the rise of crypto currencies and marijuana stocks. While these securities have provided investors with exceptional returns thus far, the potential loss which may result from a future market correction would be detrimental. Keeping this example in mind, a portfolio that strives to outperform the market index in the long run must focus on limiting the potential loss resulting from inevitable market corrections in addition to achieving above average returns during years where the market is in an upwards trend. In other words, effective portfolio management must incorporate **defensive strategies** in addition to its offensive strategies.

As mentioned, the investment community has neglected defensive strategies for far too long. For this reason, I have dedicated this entire chapter towards:

1) Explaining the significant role principal preservation has in the pursuit for long-term returns.
2) Explaining how Dividend Growth Investing encompasses various defensive mechanisms to ensure that the above average returns achieved during bull markets are protected during market corrections.

The Importance of Defense

Countless times throughout this book, the notion of maintaining a long-term focus when investing in the stock market has been expressed. The premium returns achieved in the long run are the direct result of our ability to remain patient investors during periods of short-term market fluctuations. While this practice is true, effective portfolio management entails outperforming the market index, in other words, achieving higher average returns over a long investment period. While the markets have historically recovered after a correction, a portfolio that has the ability to preserve more capital is likely to outperform the market index in the long run for the following three reasons:

1) A less significant loss during market corrections has a smaller negative effect on the long-term annual average return.
2) There is less value to "recover".
3) The Power of Compounding Interest.

We will now provide an explanation for these three points by comparing the performance of the following two portfolios:

- **Portfolio A**: A $1,000,000 portfolio that achieves a 15% annual average return during years where the market is in an upwards trend. After a market correction, the portfolio value drops by 30%.

- **Portfolio B**: A $1,000,000 portfolio that achieves a 15% annual average return during years where the market is in an upwards trend. After a market correction, the portfolio value drops by 15%.

For simplicity, I have assumed that both Portfolio A and Portfolio B start with the same beginning values and generate the same return during years where the market is moving in an upwards trend.

1) A Less Significant Loss During Market Corrections Has a Smaller Negative Effect on the Long-Term Annual Average Return

The first reason as to why capital preservation is such a vital component is straight forward: **since the percentage drop in Portfolio B is not as significant as the percentage drop in Portfolio A, the correction will have a less negative impact on Portfolio B's long-term annual average return**. For clarification, in the following chart, we have provided the 7-year annualized return of each portfolio with the assumption that over the first six years, both portfolios achieve an annual return of 15%. In the final year, both portfolios are faced with the negative consequences of a market correction.

	Y1	Y2	Y3	Y4	Y5	Y6	Y7	Annual Average Return
Portfolio A	15%	15%	15%	15%	15%	15%	-30%	8.57%
Portfolio B	15%	15%	15%	15%	15%	15%	-15%	10.71%

Figure A8: 7-Year annual average return of Portfolio A and Portfolio B.

As illustrated, being able to prevent a significant loss during a single year of negative returns increases our annual average return drastically. To continue our sports analogy, **even if our offense is simply on par with the opposing team, it is our defense that solidifies the victory**.

2) Less Value to Recover

Second, since Portfolio B dropped in value by only $150,000 versus Portfolio A, which dropped in value by $300,000, **Portfolio B will have less value to recover before returning to its initial value of $1,000,000**. An unrealized capital loss that has existed for an extensive period of time acts as a barrier to pursuing more profitable investment opportunities because many investors refuse to sell securities at a loss, but rather, are persistent in waiting for the share price to recover. Therefore, the more time a stock spends in recovery, the longer period of time the investor is locked into the same position and unable to explore alternative investment opportunities.

3) The Power of Compounding Interest

At this point, I will demonstrate how the third reason, the Power of Compound Interest, is arguably the most important motive to ensure our portfolio can limit the negative effects of market corrections on our principal. If you believe a refresher on this topic would serve as a benefit, I encourage you to revisit Chapter Three.

How does the power of compounding interest translate into preserving our principal during market corrections? To illustrate this concept, we will refer back to our previous comparison of Portfolio A and Portfolio B, only this time, we will extend our investment period. Our single investment cycle containing six years of positive returns and one year of negative returns will be extended to seven full investment cycles, bringing our investment period to 49 years. In total, the 49 years will contain 42 years of positive returns and 7 years of market corrections.

The following graph illustrates the cumulative return of both Portfolio A and Portfolio B over the entire investment period:

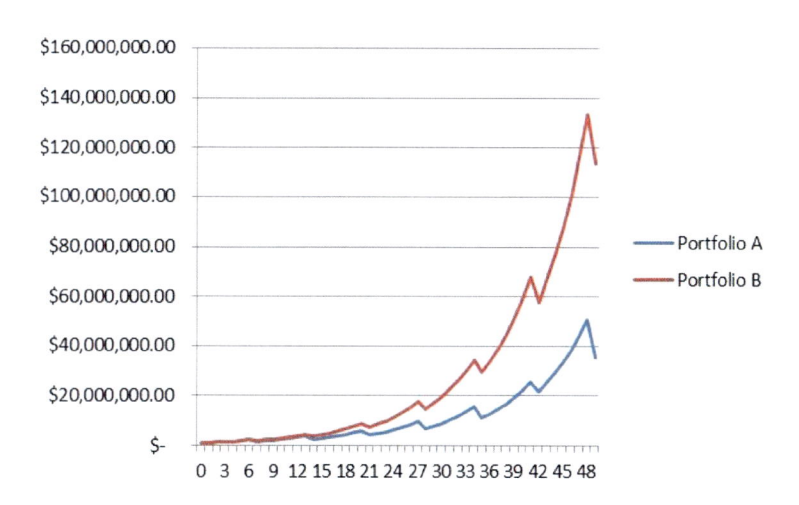

Figure B8: Growth of Portfolio A versus Portfolio B over seven investment cycles.

At the end of 49 years, Portfolio B's value grows to a total of $113,564,286, more than three times that of Portfolio A's value of $35,425,539. Remember, this incredible performance exhibited by Portfolio B was not a result of higher than average returns during periods where the market was in an upwards trend. In fact, for 42 years out of the 49-year investment period, Portfolio A and Portfolio B achieved the same 15% annual return. Portfolio B's outstanding performance was simply a direct result of its ability to preserve more capital during periods of market corrections.

For my analytical readers who would benefit from a more in-depth breakdown as to how Compound Interest played its part in our previous example, let us refer back to Year 6, the final year in which Portfolio A and Portfolio B shared the same value. At this point, just before the first market correction in Year 7, Portfolio A and B both had a value of $2,313,061. After the market correction, Portfolio A's value dropped by 30%, down to $1,619,143, and Portfolio B's value dropped by 15%, down to $1,966,102. **Even though both portfolios generated a 15% return in the year following the market correction, Portfolio B's return was greater in dollar terms because the 15% return was generated on a greater amount.** In other words, Portfolio B's 15% return in Year 8 was generated off $1,966,102 while Portfolio A's 15% return was generated off $1,619.143. While the implication of this single-year observation may at first seem minute, it quickly becomes evident just how significant an impact the power of compounding interest has on our long-term total return once we extend the investment period over a long period of time.

As shown in this example, preserving capital during market corrections is the direct result of outstanding defense and enables us to take full advantage of the power of compounding interest.

Dividend Growth Investing: The Ultimate Downside Protector

At this point, it should be very clear as to why protecting our principal during market corrections is just as important as achieving greater than average returns during bull markets. While Dividend Growth Investing has historically generated above average returns for investors during bull markets, **arguably the most important quality that has converted me to become a disciple of the investment philosophy is its ability to minimize the negative consequences associated with market corrections.**

There are two main reasons why Dividend Growth companies generally preserve more capital during market corrections than all other equity classes:

   1) The fluctuating dividend yield, and

2) The positive signal revealed as a result of a growing dividend track record.

The dividend yield is one of the most important metrics dividend investors take into account prior to making investment decisions. In short, the dividend yield represents the annual income return (cash return from dividends) the investor will receive as a percentage of the company's share price. Before the investor makes the investment, the share price is his anticipated principal value since it will be the price he pays if he chooses to make the investment. Since bond market investors view the coupon rate to determine the payments they will receive in the form of interest as a percentage of their initial investment, you can consider the dividend yield to be the stock equivalent to the coupon rate for bonds. The dividend yield equation is structured as follows:

$$\text{Dividend Yield} = \frac{\text{Annual Dividend}}{\text{Share Price}}$$

To demonstrate how the dividend yield acts as a recession-resistant mechanism, we will need to familiarize ourselves with this equation. The annual dividend that a company pays is announced prior to the dividend being paid and remains static until the company decides to increase, decrease, or cut their dividend in future periods. **Therefore, in the short run, the dividend is fixed**. For instance, if a company pays a quarterly dividend, they will usually announce the next four quarterly payments in advance of the first payment being paid. Therefore, investors are able to see the value of the dividends they will likely receive for the next year if they decide to invest in a dividend-paying company.

Unlike dividends, share prices fluctuate on a daily basis. A fluctuating share price and static dividend means that the dividend yield is negatively correlated with the company's share price. In other words, **if the share price goes up and the company does not announce a change to their dividend, the dividend yield will go down, and vice versa**.

For example, let us assume an investor would like to purchase a share in Company A because of its attractive 4% dividend yield. The share price is currently $100 and the company pays an annual dividend of $4 per share. If the share price suddenly increases to $200 and the dividend remains fixed at $4, the dividend yield will now drop to 2%. At this point, the investor may be turned off by the lower yield since they would now need to pay $200 for an annual payment of $4 instead of $100 for an annual payment of $4.

The fluctuating dividend yield is the first market correction resistant mechanism that prevents dividend-paying companies from losing a significant amount of value during bear markets. This defense mechanism can be explained in three simple steps:

> **Step 1:** In the beginning stages of a market correction, investors lose confidence and sell their dividend-paying company in an attempt to "get out" before their stock loses more value. In the short run, this nature of panic selling amongst uneducated investors applies downward force on the company's share price.
>
> **Step 2:** The sharp decrease in the share price without any change to the company's dividend causes a sharp increase in the company's dividend yield.
>
> **Step 3:** The higher dividend yield is immediately recognized by investors seeking a higher than average income yield. As a result, investors eager to take

advantage of the higher than average yield, purchase the shares of the dividend-paying company, placing upward pressure on the stock price once again.

- *Additional Information*: If a market correction is caused by a recession, the dividend yield may provide an even greater cushioning effect to a dividend-paying company's stock price. As a response to a recession, central banks generally decrease interest rates in an attempt to stimulate the economy, a tool referred to as **expansionary monetary policy**. When interest rates decrease, the coupon rates on interest-bearing securities such as bonds also decrease, thus, reducing the income stream investors can receive by investing in newly issued bonds. This reduction causes a major shift in investment capital from interest-bearing securities to dividend-paying companies since bond market investors are eager to obtain the same income yield they had prior to the interest rate decrease. **The net result is a significant inflow of capital**

into dividend-paying companies, causing upward pressure on their stock prices.

A Real World Example - The 2008 Financial Crisis

At this point, you should have a general understanding of the following concepts:

1) The significant role principal preservation plays in the pursuit of long-term investment returns.
2) Dividend Growth Investing's ability to preserve capital during bear markets as a result of fluctuating dividend yields.

To explain how the fluctuating dividend yield acts as a defensive mechanism in a real world scenario, we will compare the share price movements of the Bank of Nova Scotia, the Royal Bank of Canada, and Alphabet Inc. (Google) during the 2008 financial crisis. To compare these share price movements, we will make use of the following three pieces of information for all three companies:

- The share price in October 2007.

- The share price in the month by which the share prices had fully recovered back to their original October 2007 value.
- The length of time the company's share price took to recover.

We will use October 2007 as the base date since it is widely regarded as the beginning of the 2008 market correction.

- **Bank of Nova Scotia**
    - October 2007 share price: $53.48
    - September 2009 share price: $54.92
    - Length of time to recover: 24 months
- **Royal Bank of Canada**
    - October 2007 share price: $56.04
    - August 2009 share price: $56.45
    - Length of time to recover: 22 months
- **Alphabet Incorporated (Google)**
    - October 2007 share price: $353.84
    - September 2012 share price: $377.62
    - Length of time to recover: 59 months

As you can see from the previous example, Google's share price took more than two years longer to recover than both the Bank of Nova Scotia's share price and the Royal Bank of Canada's share price.

The differences in recovery time can be attributed to one of the two fundamental differences between both banks and the technology giant. First, Google operates in the technology market sector while the banks operate within the financial market sector. Considering the fact that the entire 2008 market correction was caused by companies within the financial sector, one would expect the recovery of the banks to be a lengthier process than that of a technology company. As we know, this was certainly not the case.

If the difference in recovery was not a result of both banks and Google operating within different market sectors, there must be a second variable at play. The second fundamental difference between the banks and Google is the reason why both the Bank of Nova Scotia and the Royal Bank of Canada were able to recover so quickly: **the fluctuating dividend yield**. Just after September 2008, the banks suffered a significant, sharp share price decrease in addition to the more gradual decrease they had already experienced from October 2007 to September 2008. However, within the three months following this sharp decrease in share prices, the share prices had recovered fairly quickly. This recovery can be attributed to the banks' decision to refrain from cutting their dividend. The combination of a static dividend with a "beat down" share price presented potential investors with a very attractive dividend yield and created an inflow of investment capital. The result was immediate upward pressure placed on the banks' stock prices, which ultimately led to a faster recovery.

With regards to Google, the company did not pay a dividend during the 2008 financial crisis. As a result, their share price was susceptible to significant losses as panic sellers sold their positions without any dividend to cushion the fall.

While the fluctuating dividend yield is the primary defensive mechanism that dividend-paying companies have to their advantage during market corrections, dividend growth companies have an indirect defense mechanism which provides even more downside protection. As mentioned in previous chapters, companies that have a proven track record of continually growing their dividends are regarded as fundamentally sound companies. By no means do these firms have any obligation to pay dividends; it is simply their choice. The act of not only paying a dividend, but continually increasing that dividend, **provides investors with the positive signal that the company has the ability to generate earnings in excess of what is required to fund future growth projects and repay debt obligations**. Therefore, a track record of continuous dividend growth is not simply a cash payment paid back to shareholders. Instead, it provides investors with the comfort that the company in which they are invested is fundamentally sound and able to weather the storm in the event of a market correction.

During market corrections, funds tend to flow into assets like gold because they are considered to be "safe havens". Fortunately for Dividend Growth companies, this trend also occurs between different companies in the stock market. Since dividends provide shareholders with not only a cash payment, but also, reassurance that the company's operations are not under any immediate risks, potential investors are motivated to transfer their wealth from companies with more ambiguous operating risks to Dividend Growth companies.

This indirect defense mechanism also played a part during the 2008 financial crisis. The decision for the Royal Bank of Canada and the Bank of Nova Scotia to maintain their dividend rather than cut their dividend sent a positive signal to investors that provided reassurance that the companies' operations were not at risk. On the other hand, companies such as Google who did not pay a dividend provided their shareholders with little reassurance. Even if Google's operations were not at risk, it was much more difficult for the company to share this information with shareholders. As a result, investor sentiment remained low and the company's share price took longer to recover.

While the investment industry focuses entirely on offensive strategies, the ultimate goal of this chapter was to emphasize the importance of focusing on defense and illustrate the recession-resistant qualities incorporated within the Dividend Growth Investing approach.

Chapter Nine
A Quantitative Approach

Between the historical evidence, financial theories, and countless real world examples provided throughout this entire book, I hope it is now evident that Dividend Growth Investing is one of the most powerful tools available to combat against the threats to our financial wealth.

While developing a strong understanding of this investment philosophy is no simple task, I believe it is surely attainable through hard work and determination. After all, there are many reputable sources, in addition to this one, that provide plenty of knowledge on the topic of Dividend Growth Investing. However, putting an investment strategy into practice is almost entirely different than simply understanding why the strategy is superior. This reminds me of a similar saying I tend to tell my daughters during times when they become overwhelmed with school: "The most important takeaway from school is not the abundance of knowledge absorbed; rather, it is the knowledge that you will be able to apply to real world scenarios."

In this chapter, my goal is to bridge the gap between:

1) Understanding the benefits of Dividend Growth Investing and,

2) Understanding how a Quantitative Approach can be used to determine which Dividend Growth companies to include in the portfolio.

In other words, this chapter will focus entirely on the application of our knowledge that we have developed over the length of this book.

Before I introduce the process, I would like to share a story about an unfortunate situation a friend of mine found himself in quite some time ago. When I was younger, I would occasionally spend an evening with a group of friends at the local casino. While gambling has never had much appeal to me, a night at the casino every so often was a fun excuse for me to spend some time with a few very close friends.

One night in particular, my friend Jim (not his real name) was consistently making winning bets at the roulette table to the point where it seemed as though he was invincible. ***He simply could not lose.*** By the end of the night, Jim was up almost 1000% on his money, leaving bystanders in utter shock. When questioned about the strategy he put to use, he simply said that *he trusted his "gut feeling"*.

After this night, Jim's view of the casino drastically changed. His abnormal success combined with the praise from bystanders caused him to believe he had somehow developed a unique ability to consistently defeat the roulette table. From that point forward, Jim began visiting the casino on his own, absolutely convinced that his intuition for choosing the right bets would guarantee him future success. From Jim's perspective, the casino was transformed from being a place to enjoy a night out with friends to an opportunity to generate a return on his money. As most of us are aware, this shift in perspective is often considered to be the first steps towards an unfortunate path of compulsive gambling.

As you may have already guessed, **Jim's success from following his "gut feeling" quickly came to an abrupt end**. After about a month of visiting the casino on his own, not only had Jim lost all of his profits from that one night of glory, sadly, he had lost roughly 50% of his savings intended as a down payment for the purchase of his first home.

The moral of Jim's story is simple: investment decisions made on the back of "gut feelings" are, in the long run, equivalent to throwing money away at a casino. "Gut feeling" strategies pose a serious threat to our ability to generate a return in the long run because they undermine the role company fundamentals should play in making investment decisions. As I have reiterated countless times throughout this book, **a company that has the ability to operate efficiently and increase earnings over a long period of time will reward shareholders in the form of share price appreciation and dividends; it is as simple as that**. To find out which companies have strong fundamentals, a deep analysis of their financial statements must be conducted since these statements provide us with a snapshot of how the company's operations have performed. **In other words, making investment decisions after interpreting the results from a financial statement analysis helps to ensure our decisions are based off company events that have already occurred rather than analyst predictions and promises made by the**

companies' management teams.

How Investment Decisions Are Made Free of "Gut Feelings" – A Quantitative Approach

To help ensure that our investment decisions are unaffected by any "gut feelings", I am a strong believer in conducting the security selection process with a quantitative approach. Quantitative analysis is the process by which companies are ranked from ideal to not ideal investments based off their ability to meet a number of pre-set investment parameters. These investment parameters should be based on company fundamentals and consistent with the Dividend Growth philosophy. For example, one possible parameter could be *% Change in latest 4 quarters Dividend vs. 1 year ago (ADIVM) is greater than or equal to 0.00.* This parameter ensures that in order for a company to be included in the portfolio, it must not only pay a dividend, but also, it must grow that dividend over time. Each company in the world of equities is analyzed and then given an overall ranking based on its ability to satisfy all of the individual investment parameters.

After the companies run through the model, the top 20 to 24 with the highest overall rankings are added to the portfolio. The following picture provides further insight on exactly how a portfolio can be constructed using a quantitative approach:

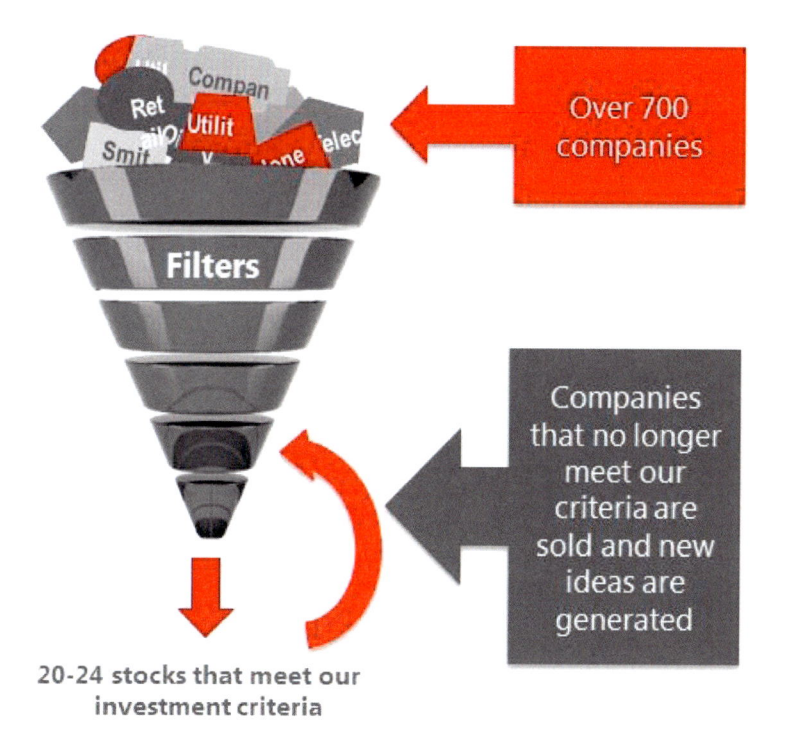

Figure A9: Illustration of Gene Giordano's Quantitative Approach.

I myself employ a Quantitative approach when selecting Dividend Growth companies for my portfolio. For my

Canadian model, I start off with roughly 700 publically traded companies trading on the Toronto Stock Exchange. From here, my quantitative model evaluates all 700 companies and ranks them from most attractive to least attractive investments based on the companies' abilities to meet my investment parameters. After the analysis is complete, the top 20 to 24 ranked companies are added to the portfolio. After the portfolio is constructed, all of the equities trading on the Toronto Stock Exchange, including the companies' in the portfolio, are continuously analyzed and ranked on a daily basis to ensure that the company fundamentals continue to satisfy my investment parameters. In the event that a company in the portfolio violates one of my investment parameters, the company is removed and replaced with the next highest-ranking company in the world of Canadian equities. My investment strategy is then proactively reviewed to incorporate current market conditions, including changes in economic and political climates.

A quantitative approach completely eliminates the risk that our investment decisions are influenced by "gut feelings" because the portfolio is constructed based off whether a company's fundamentals are in line with our

Dividend Growth parameters. If they do not fit, they are eliminated; it is as simple and straight-forward as that. This process ensures that emotions are completely removed from the investment decision and, instead, 100% of the decision is based off company fundamentals.

While quantitative analysis is the bulk of my strategy, I take a very important preliminary step prior to analyzing the 700 companies, ensuring that the 20 to 24 companies in my portfolio are the optimal choices for a Dividend Growth strategy. As you may or may not know, there have been countless occasions when companies have been caught "cooking the books". This term refers to the process by which companies intentionally omit or manipulate data on their financial statements to give a false impression of the success of their operations. The following list introduces three common tactics companies use to "spruce up" their financial statements:

- **Accelerating Revenues**: This tactic involves recording revenue on the company's financial statements before it is rightfully earned. Here are two common methods companies can use to accelerate revenues:

- o **Lump Sum Payment**: The act of recording total revenue today for a service that will be provided over a number of future periods.
- o **Channel Stuffing**: This tactic involves a manufacturing company making a large shipment to a distributor and then recording the shipment as revenue, even if the distributor has the right to return unsold merchandise back to the manufacturer. The correct way to record this transaction would be for the manufacturing company to record the shipment as an inventory. Once the distributor makes the sale, the manufacturing company should record the revenue on their financial statements.
- **Delaying Expenses**: If a company considers one of their larger expenses to be a long-term investment, they have the option of recording this expense as a capital investment. As a result, the expense is removed from the income statement and, consequently, removed from the calculation of earnings. The net result is an unjustified and manipulated boost to the company's earnings.

- **Off Balance-Sheet Items**: This tactic involves the creation of a separate legal entity that can house liabilities or incur expenses that the parent company does not want to have on its financial statements. Considering the fact that the subsidiary is a separate legal entity that is not wholly owned by the parent company, they do not have to be recorded on the parent company's financial statements and are, as a result, hidden from investors.

While "cooking the books" is most definitely illegal, it is safe to assume that many cases go unnoticed. **As a precautionary measure taken to avoid the risk of making investment decisions based off manipulated company figures, I work very closely with a third party company that standardizes and evaluates the integrity of the financial statements produced by all 700 companies.** Instead of running my quantitative model based off the company fundamentals provided by the company themselves, I run the model based off the standardized fundamentals produced by this third party company. While this extra step surely requires additional effort, I believe it is extremely important to ensure that the 20 to 24 companies suggested by my quantitative model are in fact optimal.

As I have mentioned earlier, **knowledge without application is useless**. For this reason, understanding that the many benefits of Dividend Growth Investing can only be realized if we employ a quantitative approach to portfolio management is imperative. **This approach not only safeguards that the companies in our portfolio have fundamentals that are in line with our Dividend Growth philosophy, it completely eliminates the risk that our investment decisions are based off of "gut feelings" and investor sentiment.**

Section Four:

The Conclusion

Chapter Ten

Bringing it All Together

At this point, I trust that you have developed a strong understanding of the concepts and benefits of Dividend Growth Investing as well as why we believe it is one of the most effective strategies in generating wealth over long periods of time. Considering the fact that we have covered an abundance of information throughout the course of this book, this chapter will serve as an overview of the most important concepts for your convenience.

The Threats to Our Financial Wealth and Dividend Growth Investing: When Two Titans Collide

"From the age of four, when we are first thrust into the education system, to our late 50s, the difficult working years approaching retirement, **we spend most of our lives devoted to building up our financial wealth.** *This realization poses a very serious question:* ***if we spend the majority of our life trying to build our financial wealth,***

why do we not spend an equivalent amount of time trying to protect it?" –**Gene Giordano**

I believe the most significant takeaway from this passage is that despite the clarity of its message, most of society continues to remain guilty of not taking sufficient measures to protect their hard-earned wealth.

Unfortunately, most Canadians forget the most important stage of the wealth management process because they are simply unaware of the Threats to Their Financial Wealth. If we were taught how significant an impact these threats can have in the long run, society would place a much greater emphasis on pursuing investment strategies that can combat these risks.

As a response to society's false perception of the true meaning of wealth management, I dedicated the first half of this book to explaining, in great detail, the most detrimental threats to our financial wealth:

- Understated Inflation
- Low Interest Rates
- Longevity Risk
- Taxes

- The Media
- The Investor

These threats make it clear that **the motivation for achieving long-term returns on our capital should not arise solely from the desire to simply maximize our wealth. Instead, the purpose of striving to achieve above average returns is to create a defense mechanism that will protect us from the ultimate risk: running out of money in retirement**.

In addition to society's lack of awareness with regards to the Threats to Our Financial Wealth, we have also been misled in our belief that the main path towards significant wealth creation is through employment income. **This mentality could not be farther from the truth. To truly protect ourselves against the Threats to Our Financial Wealth and generate significant sums of money over the long run, we must consider employment income to be a supplement to fuel our contributions to investment accounts.** The sooner this concept becomes evident, the sooner the investor can truly maximize the power of Dividend Growth Investing.

As reiterated countless times throughout this book, we

believe Dividend Growth Investing is the most effective strategy to protect ourselves from the many Threats to Our Financial Wealth as a result of the following four solutions:

- Enhanced Investment Returns
- Yield on Cost
- Principal Preservation
- A Quantitative Approach

I would also like to make an honorary mention to three additional solutions discussed throughout this book. These solutions are:

- The Power of Compounding Interest
- The Dividend Tax Credit
- Asset Location

The following chart summarizes a list of how each threat to our financial wealth can be eliminated through at least one of the solutions provided within this book:

Threat to Our Financial Wealth	Solution(s)
Understated Inflation	Enhanced Investment Returns
Low Interest rates	Enhanced Investment Returns
Longevity Risk	Yield on Cost The Power of Compounding Interest
Taxes	The Dividend Tax Credit Asset Location
The Media	A Quantitative Approach
The Investor	A Quantitative Approach Principal Preservation

Figure A10: Solution provided for each threat to our financial wealth.

Before we provide a summary of this chart, I would like to share an important insight regarding all six of the solutions. Throughout this book, we have referred to each solution independently in order to provide a deep understanding of how the Dividend Growth approach operates on multiple fronts. With that being said, **it should be quite evident that each solution, in fact, leads to the ultimate goal of**

generating Enhanced Investment Returns. Yield on Cost focuses on the growing investment income component of Dividend Growth Investing, which ultimately leads investors to reap Enhanced Investment Returns. Principal Preservation focuses on limiting the investor's losses during market corrections, which also leads to Enhanced Investment Returns. Dividend Growth Investing takes advantage of the Power of Compounding Interest which naturally contributes to this investment philosophy's ability to generate Enhanced Investment Returns. In addition, employing a Quantitative Approach ensures investors remain disciplined throughout the entire investment process and make investment decisions off company fundamentals rather based off emotions and investor sentiment. Investors who employ this approach are likely to also reap Enhanced Investment Returns. Even taking advantage of an effective Asset Location strategy or the Dividend Tax Credit leads to Enhanced Investment Returns since investor's can lower their overall tax liability and, consequently, achieve a higher net return.

When all is said and done, the ultimate goal for investors is to generate enough wealth that will enable them to live comfortably in retirement. To achieve this goal, investors must employ a strategy that has the capacity to generate

Enhanced Investment Returns. The Dividend Growth approach clearly possesses this capacity as illustrated through each individual solution's ability to combat against each of the Threats to Our Financial Wealth.

Understated Inflation and Low Interest Rates vs. Enhanced Investment Returns

In the second chapter of this book, we introduced the first two threats to our financial wealth: understated inflation and low interest rates. **The combined effect of understated inflation and low interest rates is detrimental to investors because our interest bearing securities, such as GICs, will not be able to keep up with the real rate of inflation; therefore, our wealth will deteriorate over time.**

Historically and on average, **companies that have grown their dividends have outperformed all other publically traded companies**. In Chapter Six titled "Enhanced Investment Returns", we displayed a graph that compared the growth of $1,000,000 from 1986 to 2016 for different companies within the world of equities.

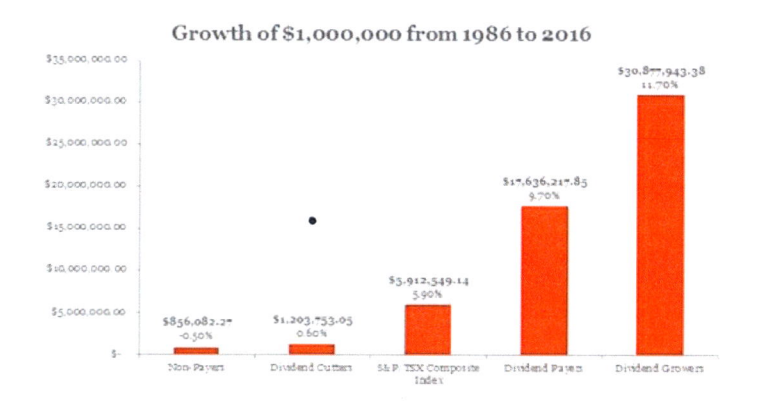

Figure B10: Growth of $1,000,000 from 1986 to 2016 for different companies within the world of equities.

As illustrated in *Figure B10*, a $1,000,000 investment in Dividend Growth Companies from 1986 to 2016, would have provided the investor with roughly $13,000,000 more than a $1,000,000 investment in companies that paid a static dividend. **These above average historical returns provide reassurance that a portfolio comprised of fundamentally sound Dividend Growth companies is likely to generate a return that is greater than the real rate of inflation.** In other words, Dividend Growth

Investing can help prevent our wealth from deteriorating over time.

To further support this point, we also compared the returns provided by Dividend Growth stocks to that provided by interest paying securities, mutual funds, and Real Estate Investing. In all three cases, the average Dividend Growth stock provided a historical return higher than that of the average interest paying security, mutual fund, and real estate property.

Longevity Risk vs. Yield on Cost and The Power of Compounding Interest

In Chapter Three, we introduced the concept of Longevity Risk, the risk of running out of money during our retirement years. Throughout the chapter, we used a number of different examples and evidence to arrive at the following conclusions:

- 1) A longer retirement period has a significant impact on our financial planning requirements.
- 2) Society's flawed view of "risk" motivates investors to believe "low risk" = "low volatility" which, in turn, makes their ability to generate a

return sufficient enough to reach the point where they have enough money to last the entirety of their retirement years even more difficult.

It should come as no surprise that a longer retirement period means investors must not only save enough money prior to retirement, they must create an indexed pension to ensure that their retirement income grows at a faster rate than the rate of inflation.

In Chapter Seven, we introduced the concept of Yield on Cost. The yield on cost ratio enables investors to evaluate how much their investment income has appreciated since the time of their initial investment.

$$Yield\ on\ Cost = \frac{Annualized\ Dividend\ or\ Interest\ in\ Most\ Recent\ Year}{Original\ Principal}$$

If you recall, we used an example of Yield on Cost to illustrate how Dividend Growth Investing can be used to create an indexed pension. Consider the following two portfolios:

- **Portfolio A**: Multiple GICs which provide the investor with a fixed interest rate, guaranteed

principal repayment, and a predetermined investment period.
- **Portfolio B**: Multiple Dividend Growth companies that provide the investor with a growing income stream, the potential for share price appreciation, and an unrestricted investment period.

Despite the fact that Portfolio B is more favourable than Portfolio A on multiple fronts, it is the rising income stream that should be regarded as the greatest advantage. With GICs, since the interest payments received by an investor remains static over the entire investment period, the investor's purchasing power diminishes over time after accounting for the effects of inflation. However, with Dividend Growth Investing, the investor can help eliminate the risk of outliving their retirement savings contingent on the following two factors:

- The company's ability to grow their dividends at a rate faster than the rate of inflation, and,
- A dividend income high enough to fund the investor's expenses in retirement.

If both factors are satisfied, the investor's risk of outliving their retirement savings is completely eliminated, regardless of the length of the retirement period. **The investor would never need to tap into their retirement savings since their income from dividends alone would be large enough to fund their lifestyle expenses and would not diminish as a result of inflation since the dividends would be growing at a faster rate**. In other words, in this example, the investor would have successfully created an indexed pension through Dividend Growth Investing.

In addition to Yield on Cost, we introduced an investment tool that transforms "Longevity" from a threat to our financial wealth to a supplement; **The Power of Compounding Interest**. In order for an investor to take advantage of this solution, we explained that the investor must first disregard society's flawed view that "low risk" equals "low volatility" since investments that have the ability to maximize long run returns generated through compound interest are generally more volatile. While obtaining a high Yield on Cost ensures an investor's income in retirement grows at a rate faster than inflation and, consequently, ensures the investor's income is sufficient enough to fund their lifestyle expenses, the Power of Compound Interest helps investors save enough wealth prior to beginning their retirement. To explain this solution, we first provided definitions for both Simple Interest and Compound Interest:

- **Simple Interest**: The percentage return generated by a security is based off the investor's original principal.
- **Compound Interest**: The percentage return generated by a security is based off the investor's original principal plus all previously generated returns.

The main difference between Simple Interest and Compound interest is the fact that returns generated by compound interest enabled securities compound off of all of the wealth accumulated through previous returns in addition to the original principal.

At this point, we compared the dollar returns of a simple interest yielding security to a compound interest yielding security:

- **Security A – Simple Interest**
    - $100,000 invested in a 5.6% yielding GIC.
- **Security B – Compound Interest**

- $100,000 invested in the Canadian stock market yielding an annual average return of 5.6%.

If you recall, the results were beyond outstanding. **After 50 years, the 5.6% annual compounded return provided by the Canadian stock market generated an astounding $1,144,740.41 more than the 5.6% annual simple return provided by the GIC**. In percentage terms, the stock market generated a 1425% return whereas the GIC generated a relatively pathetic 280% return.

This simple, yet powerful, example validated the notion that the longer the time period a compound interest security has to compound, the larger the annual dollar returns will become.

Investors who choose to disregard society's false notion that volatile securities should be considered "high risk" will truly be able to take advantage of compound interest. In doing so, the true risk to their financial wealth, not saving enough money to last for the entirety of their retirement years, will be minimized.

While Longevity Risk poses a significant threat to our financial wealth, it is quite evident that Yield on Cost and the Power of Compound Interest are effective solutions that mitigate the negative effects.

Taxes vs. the Dividend Tax Credit and Asset Location

In Chapter Four, we introduced the negative effect of taxes on our investment returns. Unfortunately, it is impossible to completely eliminate taxes since the government will always expect to receive a portion of our hard earned wealth. While we cannot eliminate this threat entirely, in Chapter Four, we illustrated multiple strategies as to how we can minimize this liability.

First, we compared the tax liability structure for interest paying securities, dividend paying securities, and taxes charged on capital gains. This information has been summarized in the following chart:

	Interest Income	**Dividend Income**	**Capital Gains**
Tax Liability Control	Subject to the interest payment schedule chosen by the issuing institution. The investor has zero control.	Subject to the dividend payment schedule chosen by the company's board of directors. The investor has zero control.	Subject to the point at which the investor decides to sell his or her securities. The investor has complete control.
Magnitude of Tax Liability	Taxed at the investor's marginal tax rate with no preferential tax treatment. This form of taxation results in the highest tax liability.	Taxed at the investor's marginal tax rate with preferential tax treatment. The investor receives a dividend tax credit to reduce their overall tax liability. This form of taxation results in a lower tax liability than interest income, but higher tax liability than capital gains.	50% of the investor's capital gains is taxed at the investor's marginal tax rate. This form of taxation results in the lowest tax liability.

Figure C10: Characteristics of tax liabilities for interest income, dividend income, and capital gains.

As illustrated in the previous chart, it is very clear that taxes charged on capital gains receive the largest break. Not only do investors maintain control over the timing of their tax liability, the magnitude of the tax liability is also significantly lower. With that being said, while dividend and interest seeking investors both do not have any control over the timing of their tax liability, the magnitude of the tax charged on dividend income is lower than that charged on interest income as a result of The Dividend Tax Credit provided to shareholders in dividend paying companies. This preferential tax treatment is an initiative by the government to motivate investment in Canadian companies. In addition, since companies pay dividends from after-tax profits, in other words, the dividends have already been taxed at the corporate level, the Dividend Tax Credit aims to eliminate double taxation.

In addition to the Dividend Tax Credit, investors have the ability to minimize their tax liability by utilizing an effective Asset Location strategy. This strategy involves the allocation of asset classes to a specific account type that will ultimately minimize the portfolio's overall tax liability. In Chapter Four, we explained how investors can reduce their overall tax liability through making proper use of the following three account types:

- 1) Non-Registered
- 2) Registered Retirement Savings Plan (RRSP)
- 3) Tax-Free Savings Plan (TFSA)

The following chart illustrates the level of priority to be given to each security type for each account type in order to minimize the investor's overall tax liability:

Account Type	1st Priority	2nd Priority	3rd Priority
Non-Registered	Non-Income Producing Securities	Dividend Paying Securities	Interest Paying Securities
Registered Retirement Savings Plan (RRSP)	Interest Paying Securities	Dividend Paying Securities	Non-Income Producing Securities
Tax-Free Savings Account	Interest Paying Securities	Dividend Paying Securities	Non-Income Producing Securities

Figure D10: Level of priority to be given to each security type for each account type in order to minimize the investor's overall tax liability.

For an explanation as to why this priority scale results in the most tax efficient outcome for the investor, I encourage you to revisit Chapter Four.

The Media and the Investor vs. A Quantitative Approach

In Chapter Five, we explained how the concept of **purchasing fundamentally sound companies at a discount** does not resonate well with the investment community. When prices are increasing, investors are more than willing to invest in an attempt to 'join in on the rally'. When prices are decreasing, investors panic and sell their positions out of fear that prices will continue to decrease. This reversed philosophy of buying when prices are high and selling when prices are low is not only flawed, it also has the potential to be incredibly destructive to our financial wealth. Unfortunately, this flawed concept has slowly transitioned to become a norm in the investment community as a result of the following:

- 1) An injustice committed by the Investment Media to cover topics that will maximize profit rather than properly inform investors.
- 2) Lack of responsibility from investors to keep themselves informed and follow a basic rule of thumb; all else equal, high prices are bad and low prices are good.

In Chapter Nine, we discussed how employing a quantitative approach to investing ensures that our investment decisions are unaffected by emotions and the opinions of others. Quantitative analysis is the process by which companies are ranked from ideal to not ideal investments based on their ability to meet a number of pre-set investment parameters. The top 20 to 24 companies that best satisfy the investment parameters are then added to the portfolio. When combined with a Dividend Growth philosophy, the parameters are constructed in a way that ensures only companies with sound fundamentals and a proven track record of dividend growth will enter the portfolio.

A quantitative approach completely eliminates the risk that our investment decisions are influenced by emotions and the opinions of others because the portfolio is constructed based on whether a company's fundamentals are in line with the investment parameters. If they do not fit, they are eliminated; it is as simple and straightforward as that. This process helps ensure that emotions are completely removed from the investment decision and, instead, 100% of the decision is based on company fundamentals.

The Investor vs. Principal Preservation

In the previous subsection, we mentioned how one of the many flawed concepts accepted by the investment industry is the notion of buying when prices are rising and selling when prices are decreasing. One reason as to why this concept has been accepted for so many years is the result of a lack of responsibility from investors to keep themselves informed and follow a basic rule of thumb; **all else equal, high prices are bad and low prices are good**. When stocks decrease in price as a result of factors unrelated to the underlying company's fundamentals, investors should view this as an opportunity to increase their position in good, strong companies at a discounted price. The temporary decrease in the value of our portfolio is simply the price we pay for premium returns in the long run.

With that being said, in the event of a significant market correction, one resulting in losses in excess of twenty percent, it is very unreasonable to expect investors to remain perfectly calm and collected. In fact, in this scenario, many investors would end up selling their securities out of fear that their investments will continue to drop in value.

In the previous subsection, we explained how a Quantitative Approach completely eliminates the threat of the Investor making investment decisions based off emotions because the portfolio is constructed based on whether a company's fundamentals are in line with the investment parameters. In the event of a severe market correction, Dividend Growth Investing can reduce the probability that an investor ends up making an investment decision from an emotional standpoint because of its Principal Preservation qualities.

As mentioned in Chapter Eight, the most influencing factor that has motivated me to become a disciple of Dividend Growth Investing is the recession resistant qualities that it incorporates.

There are two main reasons why Dividend Growth companies generally preserve more capital during market corrections than all other equity classes:

- **1) The fluctuating dividend yield**
- **2) The positive signal released from a growing dividend track record**

As we now know, the dividend yield is one of the most important metrics dividend investors consider when making investment decisions. In short, the dividend yield tells investors the return they will receive in the form of a dividend as a percentage of the company's share price. Before the investor makes the investment, the share price is their anticipated principal value since it will be the price they pay if they choose to make the investment. As a reminder, the equation is as follows:

$$\text{Dividend Yield} = \frac{\text{Annual Dividend}}{\text{Share Price}}$$

The fluctuating dividend yield is what prevents dividend-paying companies from losing a significant amount of value during market corrections. This defense mechanism can be explained in three simple steps:

- **Step 1)**: Once a market correction is underway, investors lose confidence and sell their dividend-paying company in an attempt to "get out" before their stock loses more value. This nature of panic selling amongst uneducated investors applies downward force on the company's share price in the short run.

- **Step 2)**: The sharp decrease in the share price without any change to the company's dividend causes a sharp increase in the company's dividend yield.
- **Step 3)**: The higher dividend yield is immediately recognized by investors seeking a higher than average income yield. As a result, investors eager to take advantage of the higher than average yield purchase the shares of the dividend-paying company, placing upward pressure on the stock price once again.

While the dividend yield is the primary defensive mechanism that dividend-paying companies have to their advantage during market corrections, Dividend Growth companies have an indirect defense mechanism which provides even more downside protection. As mentioned throughout this book, companies that have a proven track record of continuously growing their dividends are regarded as fundamentally sound companies. By no means do these firms have any obligation to pay dividends; it is simply their choice. **Continuously increasing their dividend, let alone simply paying a dividend, provides investors with the positive signal that the company has the ability to generate earnings in excess of what is required to fund future growth projects and repay debt obligations**. Therefore, a track record of continuous dividend growth is not simply a cash payment paid back to shareholders. Instead, it provides investors with the comfort of knowing that the company in which they are invested is fundamentally sound and better able to weather the storm in the event of a market correction.

During market corrections, funds tend to flow into assets like gold because they are considered to be "safe havens." Fortunately for dividend growth companies, this trend also occurs between different companies in the stock market. Since dividends provide shareholders with not only a cash payment, but also reassurance that the company's operations are not under any immediate risks, potential investors are motivated to transfer their wealth to dividend growth companies from companies with more ambiguous operating risks.

By limiting the amount of principal lost during a significant bear market, investors are less likely to act on emotions and sell their positions while prices are decreasing.

Concluding Thoughts

I truly hope this book has provided you with a deeper understanding of the many benefits Dividend Growth Investing has to offer and why we consider it to be the most powerful wealth creation strategy available to investors. I would like to end off with this final message:

The above average returns generated from Dividend Growth Investing can only be achieved by maintaining a long-term focus, disregarding short-term market fluctuations, and investing in fundamentally sound companies with a proven track record of consistent dividend growth. By employing a Dividend Growth approach and understanding the concept that employment income should be used to fuel contributions to investment accounts, your journey towards achieving financial freedom just became significantly shorter.

References

[i] Arnott, Robert D. and Asness, Cliff S., Does Dividend Policy Foretell Earnings Growth? (December 2001). Available at SSRN: https://ssrn.com/abstract=295974 or http://dx.doi.org/10.2139/ssrn.295974

[ii] DST Systems, Inc. (2017). In volatile markets investors may find comfort in dividends. Retrieved from https://www.merrilledge.com/article/in-volatile-markets-investors-may-find-comfort-in-dividends

[iii] Watson, W. (2018, November 09). The Bank of Canada gives itself an A- for forecasting. Retrieved from https://www.fraserinstitute.org/blogs/the-bank-of-canada-gives-itself-an-a-for-forecasting

[iv]
- Coffee Prices - 45 Year Historical Chart. (n.d.). Retrieved from http://www.macrotrends.net/2535/coffee-prices-historical-chart-data
- HPI Tool. (n.d.). Retrieved from http://www.crea.ca/housing-market-stats/mls-home-price-index/hpi-tool/
- Historical electricity rates. (n.d.). Retrieved from https://www.oeb.ca/rates-and-your-bill/electricity-rates/historical-electricity-rates
- Consumer Price Index, 2000 to Present. (n.d.). Retrieved from http://www.bankofcanada.ca/rates/price-indexes/cpi/
- Statistics Canada. (2018). Canadian and international tuition fees by level of study. Retrieved from https://www150.statcan.gc.ca/t1/tbl1/en/tv.action?pid=3710004501, Table: 37-10-0045-01 (formerly CANSIM 477-0077)
- Canadian Postal Rates. (n.d.). Retrieved from https://adminware.ca/checklist/chk_rate.htm

[v] Cleveland Clinic. (2016, October 26). Cleveland Clinic Unveils Top 10 Medical Innovations Most Likely To Be Game Changers. Retrieved

from https://newsroom.clevelandclinic.org/2016/10/26/cleveland-clinic-unveils-top-10-medical-innovations-likley-game-changers/

[vi]Statistics Canada. (2018, May 17). Life expectancy, 1920?1922 to 2009?2011. Retrieved from https://www150.statcan.gc.ca/n1/pub/11-630-x/11-630-x2016002-eng.htm

[vii]Tangerine Bank. (n.d.). Historical rates. Retrieved from https://www.tangerine.ca/en/rates/historical-rates/index.html

[viii]TaxTips.ca. (n.d.). Ontario 2019 and 2018 Personal Marginal Income Tax Rates. Retrieved from https://www.taxtips.ca/taxrates/on.htm

[ix]TaxTips.ca. (n.d.). Ontario 2019 and 2018 Personal Marginal Income Tax Rates. Retrieved from https://www.taxtips.ca/taxrates/on.htm

[x]TaxTips.ca. (n.d.). Federal & Provincial/Territorial Enhanced Dividend Tax Credit Rates. Retrieved from https://www.taxtips.ca/dtc/enhanceddtc/enhanceddtcrates.htm

[xi]Rotfleisch, D. (2018, February 14). Canada: Dividend Gross-Up And Dividend Tax Credits - A Toronto Tax Lawyer Analysis. Retrieved from http://www.mondaq.com/canada/x/673328/Corporate+Tax/Dividend+GrossUp+and+Dividend+Tax+Credits+A+Toronto+Tax+Lawyer+Analysis

[xii]Canada Revenue Agency. (2019, January 25). Contributions. Retrieved from https://www.canada.ca/en/revenue-agency/services/tax/individuals/topics/tax-free-savings-account/contributions.html

[xiii]Trussler, M., & Soroka, S. (2014). Consumer Demand for Cynical and Negative News Frames. *The International Journal of Press/Politics, 19*(3), 360-379. doi:10.1177/1940161214524832

[xiv]Martino, B. D. (2006). Frames, Biases, and Rational Decision-Making in the Human Brain. *Science, 313*(5787), 684-687. doi:10.1126/science.1128356

[xv]Bourne, D. (2017, April). The power of dividends – offering a winning strategy. *Dividends*, *1*, 1-2. Retrieved from https://ca.rbcwealthmanagement.com/documents/258147/258168/Power+of+Dividends+(April+2017).pdf/981d1571-1dd8-4b1e-8609-5da404e66a01

[xvi]Carrick, R. (2018, June 19). Table: Rob Carrick evaluates Canada's 100 largest mutual funds. Retrieved from https://www.theglobeandmail.com/investing/markets/inside-the-market/article-table-rob-carrick-evaluates-canadas-100-largest-mutual-funds/

[xvii]Segal, J. (2019, January 09). Value Investing Vet Mason Hawkins Steps Down. Retrieved from https://www.institutionalinvestor.com/article/b1cmcbzmg3z7tz/Value-Investing-Vet-Mason-Hawkins-Steps-Down

[xviii]O'Rielly, W., CFA, & Preisano, M., CFA. (2000, January 01). Dealing With The Active. Retrieved from https://www.etf.com/publications/journalofindexes/joi-articles/1159.html

[xix]Toronto Real Estate Board. (n.d.). [Toronto MLS Sales and Average Price]. Unpublished raw data.

Made in the USA
Lexington, KY
25 March 2019